Microservices Practitioner Guide

Gopala Krishna Behara
Tirumala Khandrika

MK
Meghan-Kiffer Press
Tampa, Florida, USA
www.mkpress.com
Innovation at the Intersection of Business and Technology

Cover Picture: Vincent van Gogh, *The Starry Night*

Complementary Book:

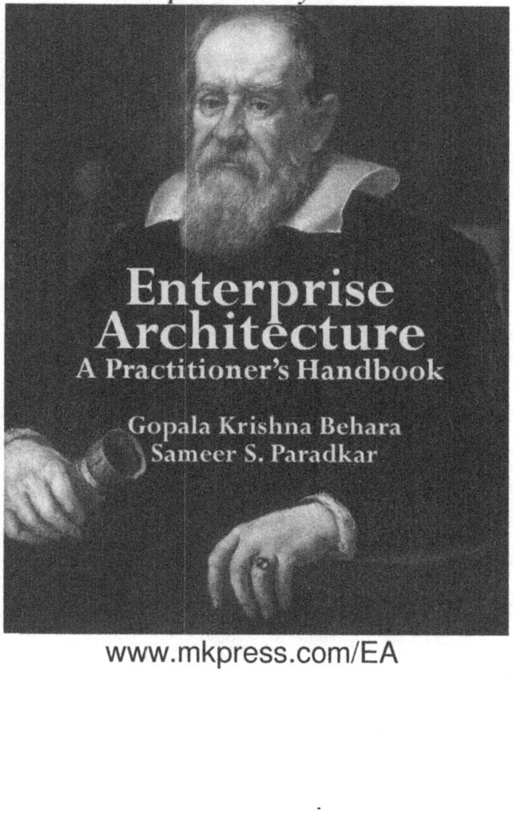

www.mkpress.com/EA

ISBN 10: 0-929652-62-2 ISBN-13: 978-0-929652-62-7

Published by Meghan-Kiffer Press
310 East Fern Street — Suite G
Tampa, FL 33604 USA

Meghan-Kiffer books are available at special quantity discounts for corporate education and training use. For more information write Special Sales, Meghan-Kiffer Press, Suite G, 310 East Fern Street, Tampa, Florida 33604 or email orders@mkpress.com

MK

Meghan-Kiffer Press
Tampa, Florida, USA
Innovation at the Intersection of Business and Technology

Printed in the United States of America. SAN 249-7980
MK Printing 10 9 8 7 6 5 4 3 2 1

Table of Contents

Preface

Microservices is an architectural style in which large, complex software applications are composed of one or more smaller services. Each of these Microservices focuses on completing one task that represents a small business capability. These Microservices can be developed in any programming language.

This reference guide consolidates author's experience of many projects and programs with customers, and insights from many hours of intense discussions with experts from client companies and consultancies. The book takes a holistic view of the Microservices Architecture, while also giving specific guidelines on how to establish and roll out future-state Microservices Architecture based on the methodology and approach documented in this reference guide.

Software professionals interested in learning about Microservices and how to develop or redesign a monolithic application using Microservices can benefit from this book.

—Gopala Krishna Behara

—Tirumala Khandrika

July 2018

Acknowledgements

We thank our discussion partners, reviewers and supporters, whose valuable comments and feedback have greatly contributed to this book. We look forward to your feedback and valuable inputs on an on-going basis.

We would like to thank our family members and friends for their encouragement and constant support during the development of the book.

1. Introduction

1.1. Overview

The term "micro web services" was first used by Dr. Peter Rogers during a conference on cloud computing in 2005. "Microservices" themselves premiered at an event for software architects in 2011, where the term used to describe a style of architecture that many attendees were experimenting with at the time. Netflix and Amazon were among the early pioneers of Microservices. The popularity of Microservices has recently been on the rise because they can solve many current IT challenges such as increasing speed, scalability of applications and rapid test processes.

In software development, smaller is usually better. More minor things are easier to code, easier to maintain, simpler to test, and easier to deploy. Systems built this way can be more scalable, more flexible, and deliver value with greater speed. Microservices supports this kind of development.

Microservices is a method of developing software applications as a suite of independently deployable, small, modular services in which each service runs a unique process and communicates through a well-defined, lightweight mechanism to serve a business goal.

Adoption of Microservices Architecture requires an enterprise to undergo changes across various areas. The Major changes are,

i. Organizational Cultural Changes
ii. Architectural Changes
iii. Operational Changes
iv. Governance Changes

Below diagram describes the changes in details.

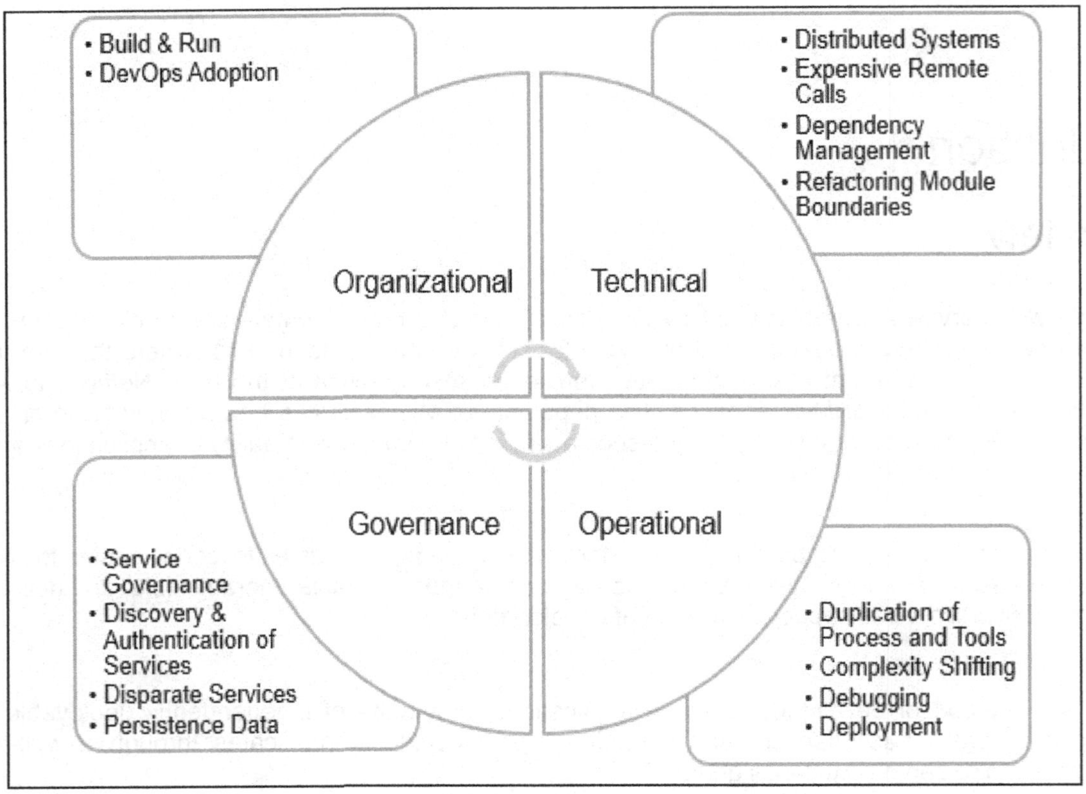

Changes affecting the Enterprise

Today, enterprises are adopting technologies like Analytics, Mobility, Social media, IoT and Smart embedded devices to change customer relationships, internal processes and value propositions. Microservices acts as building blocks for building modern distributed enterprise systems.

Microservices provides the agility, reliability, maintainability, scalability and deploy ability that aid enterprises through their digital transformation process. It helps the enterprise in achieving the following factors,

- Focus on Business Need
- Agility, enterprises can introduce new products or enhancements into the market quickly
- Enhancing the customer experience
- Reliability, if a service is down, the customer will not be able to use the functionality provided by that specific service, but the rest of the system is still usable
- Scalability, the system can be configured to auto-scale (up / out) and during off-peak hours, it can go back to its normal configuration resulting in a better customer experience and cost-savings for the customer
- Can be developed & deployed independently of other services

What is Microservice

Microservices is an architecture style, in which software systems or applications are composed of one or more independent and self-contained services. It is not a product, framework, or platform. It is a strategy for building large distributed systems. Microservices are loosely coupled and deployed independently of one another.

While there is not one single definition for the term "Microservice," the below two are very helpful,
Microservices are small, autonomous services that work together —Sam Newman, Thoughtworks
Loosely coupled service-oriented architecture with bounded contexts —Adrian Cockcroft, Battery Ventures

1.2. Monolithic Vs Microservices Applications

A monolithic application is an application where all of the logic runs in a single application server. Typical monolithic applications are large and built by multiple teams, requiring careful orchestration of deployment for every change. We also consider applications monolithic if, while there are multiple API services providing the business logic, the entire presentation layer is a single large web app.

The following diagram depicts the typical Monolithic application

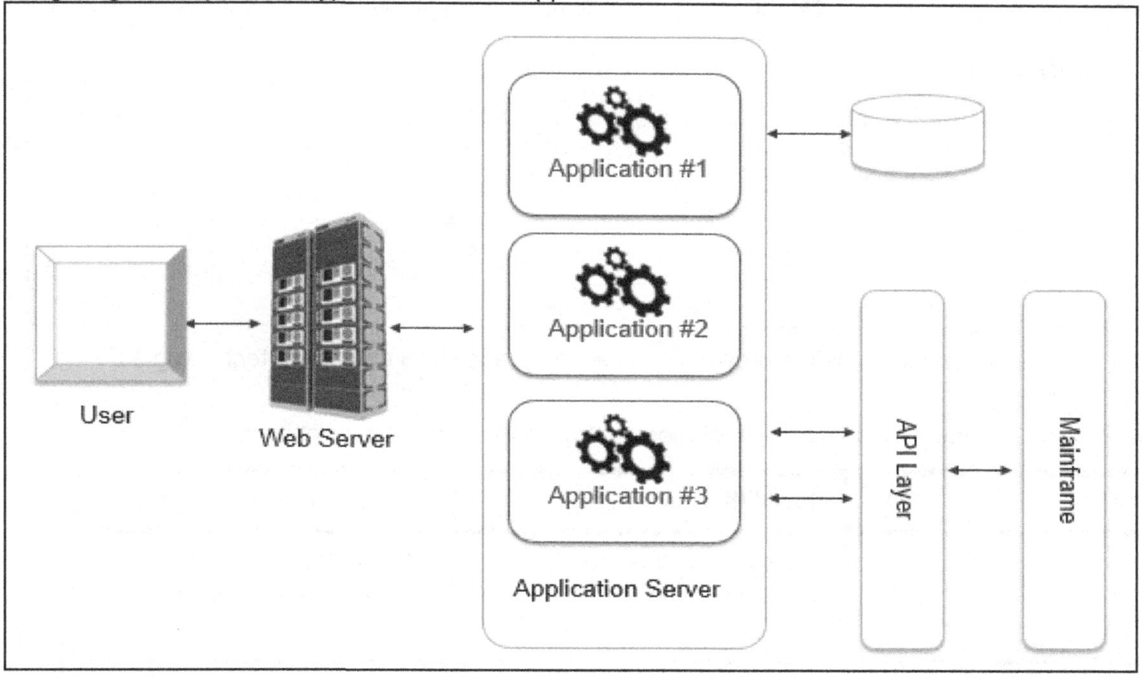

Monolithic applications with a multi-tiered architecture

Large monolithic applications typically have a large application code base, which is often Intimidating to developers. It is not always intuitive what part of the application code needs modification for a specific feature request or a change request. This leads to a larger learning curve for on boarding developers, increases project delivery timeline, and reduces rates of enhancement and delivery of new capabilities. Monolithic applications often have a large business scope and many IT infrastructure touch points. Any change to the application results in multiple reviews and approvals, resulting in increased deployment cycle times.

Microservice applications allow developers break down their work into smaller Independent teams, and to integrate that work delivered. Microservices recommends to have smaller focused teams that align with business revenue and cost centers. This enables business owners to see resource allocation, and to move them from low impact business areas to new or higher impact business areas.

Efficiency is achieved, by automating deployment, logging, and monitoring practices across multiple Microservice project teams. Customers interviewed expect to realize a cost savings of 3 to 1 by automating much of the infrastructure and platform as a service (PaaS).

Below Figure shows a Microservices architecture with multiple languages and data store technologies.

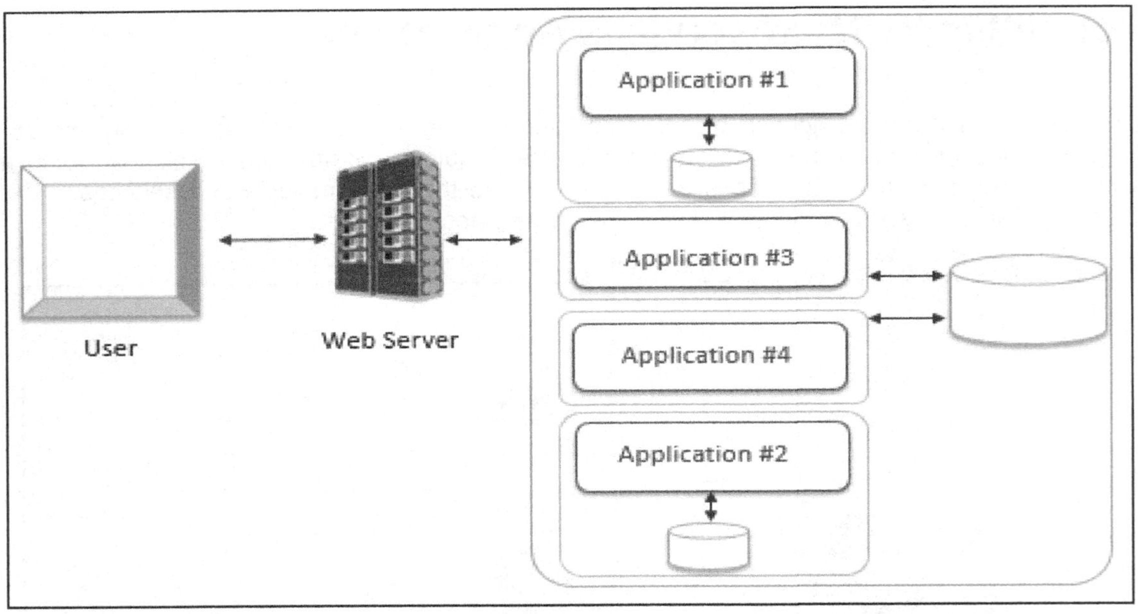

Microservices architecture with multiple languages and data store technologies

The following table provides the comparison of Monolithic and Microservices Architectures.

Category	Monolithic architecture	Microservices architecture
Code	A single code base for the entire application.	Multiple code bases. Each microservice has its own code base.
Understandability	Often confusing and hard to maintain.	Much better readability and much easier to maintain.
Deployment	Complex deployments with maintenance windows and scheduled downtimes.	Simple deployment as each microservice can be deployed individually, with minimal if not zero downtime.
Language	Typically entirely developed in one programming language.	Each microservice can be developed in a different programming language.
Scaling	Requires you to scale the entire application even though bottlenecks are localized.	Enables you to scale bottle-necked services without scaling the entire application.

1.3. Elements of Microservices

Microservices can be developed in any programming language, each running in its own process and communicating with lightweight mechanisms like HTTP resource API such as REST. Each Microservices focuses on completing one task and that one task represents a small business capability. There exist no criteria on how small a Microservice must be. These services lead the application decomposition into smaller pieces. This helps to scale up parts of applications rather than scaling up the entire application. The below diagram depicts the major characteristics of Microservices which are classified as,

- Business
- Technology
- Process
- People

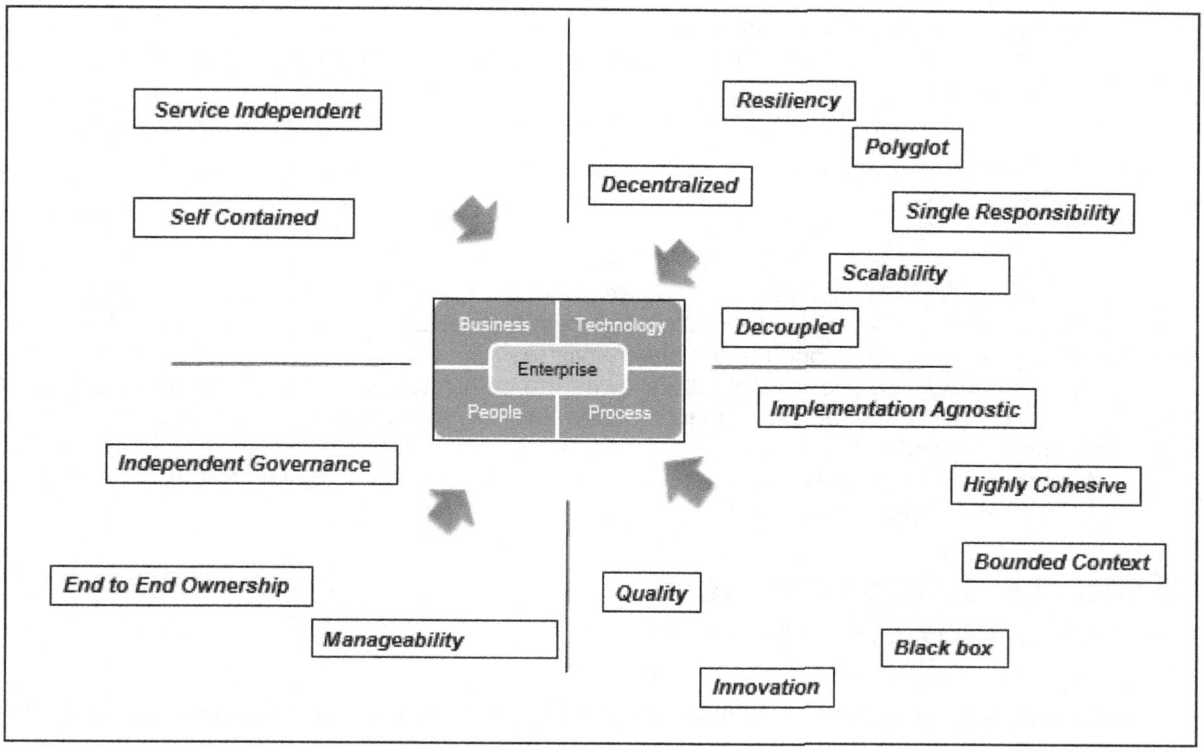

Elements of Microservices

- Business
    - Service Independent: As Microservices are autonomous, each Microservice can change in its lifecycle in an independent manner with other services.
    - Self-Contained: Services are easily replaceable and upgradeable. It promotes single ownership of the service. To achieve self-containment proper granularity in decomposition is essential

- Technology
    - Decentralized: Microservices decentralizes architectures, patterns, languages, standards, component & data responsibility and governance because of its architectural style.
    - Resiliency. If one of the Microservices goes down, it won't necessarily bring the whole application down as it would with a monolithic
    - Polyglot: Microservices architecture supports multiple technologies, to be specific, a technology that is most fit for the purpose.
    - Single Responsibility: A Service is aligned to a single business activity and is responsible for that business activity and deliver the complete business logic necessary to fulfill the business activity
    - Scalability: Microservices can be deployed and scaled independently of each other.
    - Decoupled: Microservice should implement a single atomic business function. This helps in maintaining minimum dependency on other services
- Process

- Implementation Agnostic: Implementation shall support multiple development platforms and technologies and can be deployed in any of the containers
- Blackbox: Microservice shall be a black box (no internal details will be exposed outside the service boundary) for other components / systems using / invoking it.
- Bounded Context: This is one of the important characteristic of Microservices. Other services do not need to know anything about underlying implementation or architecture of other Microservices.
- Innovation. New versions of small independent services can be deployed more rapidly, making it easier to experiment and innovate.
- Quality: Composability and responsibility, more maintainable code, better scaling and optimization

- People
  - End-to-End Ownership: This is a cultural shift for the project team. The development team will maintain each project built using Microservices architecture as opposed to the regular practice (of handing it over to the support and maintenance team).
  - Independent Governance: Single team owns the complete ownership of the Microservice life cycle. This team owns the all the aspects of the Microservices including governance. Governance is decentralized and autonomous.
  - Manageability. Smaller Microservices code bases are easier for developers to understand, making changes and deployments easier

1.4. Features of Microservices

The following are the features of the Microservices,

- Decoupling: Services within a system are largely decoupled and can therefore be easily built, altered and scaled
- Componentization: Microservices are independent components that can easily be replaced or upgraded.
- Business Capabilities: Microservices are very simple and focus on a single business capability.
- Autonomy: Many developers and teams can work independently of each other and thus significantly increase speed.
- Continuous Delivery: Allows frequent releases through systematic automation of software creation, testing and approval.
- Responsibility: Microservices do not focus on software projects; instead they treat applications as products for which they are responsible.
- Decentralized Governance: The focus is on using the right tool for the job, not on standardizing technology platforms. Teams prefer to develop useful tools that other developers can use to solve similar problems
- Agility: Microservices support agile development. A new feature the customer does not yet quite believe will be successful cannot only be quickly developed—it can also be quickly discarded again

1.5. Basic Rules on the Usage of Microservices

Microservices are not a silver bullet. By implementing them communication, teamwork, and other problems that may have been previously implicit are now exposed. In a Microservice architecture, the services tend to get simpler, but the architecture tends to get more complex. That complexity is often managed with tooling, automation, and process.

As with anything else, whether or not Microservice architecture is right for enterprise depends on the requirements, because they all have their pros and cons. The quick pros and cons of adoption of Microservices are listed below,

Pros

- Microservice architecture gives developers the freedom to independently develop and deploy services
- A Microservice can be developed by a fairly small team
- Code for different services can be written in different languages (though many practitioners discourage it)
- Easy integration and automatic deployment (using open-source continuous integration tools such as Jenkins, Hudson, etc.)
- Easy to understand and modify for developers, thus can help a new team member become productive quickly
- The developers can make use of the latest technologies
- The code is organized around business capabilities
- Starts the web container more quickly, so the deployment is also faster
- When change is required in a certain part of the application, only the related service can be modified and redeployed—no need to modify and redeploy the entire application
- Better fault isolation: if one Microservice fails, the other will continue to work (although one problematic area of a monolith application can jeopardize the entire system)
- Easy to scale and integrate with third-party services
- No long-term commitment to technology stack

Cons

- Due to distributed deployment, testing can become complicated and tedious
- Increasing number of services can result in information barriers
- The architecture brings additional complexity as the developers have to mitigate fault tolerance, network latency, and deal with a variety of message formats as well as load balancing
- Being a distributed system, it can result in duplication of effort
- When number of services increases, integration and managing whole products can become complicated
- In addition to several complexities of monolithic architecture, the developers have to deal with the additional complexity of a distributed system
- Developers have to put additional effort into implementing the mechanism of communication between the services
- Handling use cases that span more than one service without using distributed transactions is not only tough but also requires communication and cooperation between different teams
- The architecture usually results in increased memory consumption
- Partitioning the application into Microservices is very much an art

1.6. When to do Microservices

Microservices can't be achieved by focusing on a particular set of patterns, process, or tools. The real value of Microservices is realized with two key aspects—speed and safety. Every single decision about software development ends up as a trade-off that impacts these two ideals. Finding an effective balance between them at scale is what we call the Microservices way.

The following are the factors, which drive the enterprise to use Microservices as their solution.

- Development for cloud based systems. Ie when enterprise decides to move from traditional SOA to cloud based applications, Microservices are preferred
- To develop highly distributed systems
- When the enterprise primary business revolves around extremely high volume transactions
- If the functionality to be highly available. Deploy the functionality as service in multiple, redundant providers so that some are available even when others are not.
- For the solutions that require the integration of business capability from disparate systems and programming models
- For aligning business and IT functionality
- For business and technology agility
- Better ROI
- For incremental development (Agile) and continuous deployment of business software

1.7. When not to do Microservices

The following are the factors, which negates the usage of Microservices.

- Scenarios where monolithic and centralized application architecture make more sense (for more simple, small and low available application development)
- For applications where consistency is high priority over eventual consistency
- Small enterprises with homogeneous network and technology confined to the single vendor.
- Scenarios where standards based integration not needed. The solution might be simple data exchange between applications and external systems.
- When there is no frequent release because of changing requirements
- Non cloud based development
- Re-Architecting data platforms. If service relies upon a system of record (Mainframe, Oracle database, SAP system, and others), then Microservices do not fit the definition.
- Scenarios where there is no product like ownership is required from the project teams
- Cultural shift in enterprise in terms of team autonomy, long-term commitment to a technical / product stack is not possible or required.

1.8. Benefits of Microservices

Microservices are build using lightweight framework, open source technologies. It offers quick time to market.

- Improves fault isolation, larger applications can remain largely unaffected by the failure of a single module.
- Provides business agility, supports Continuous Delivery. New Functionality can be added easily and quickly. Development teams work independently
- Eliminates long-term commitment to a single technology stack, develop the code independently using whatever technology the developer feels right for delivering business function. Different part of systems can use different technology stack if needed for better performance. Technology heterogeneity or polyglot programming is one essential benefit of Microservices.

- Developer perspective, makes it easier for a new developer to understand the functionality of a service
- Smaller codebases help developers focus and have a higher empathic relationship with the users of their product, leading to a better motivation and clarity in their work
- Ease of deployment, one part of the system can move to another machine or to another cloud while rest of the service could stay on premise

1.9. Summary

This chapter narrates the situations, when to use Microservices and when not to use. Recommendation of usage of Microservices at the enterprise level are described in this chapter. Adoption of Microservices by an enterprise provides the extreme time to Market and establishes the bridge between Business and IT of the enterprise. Microservices implementation provides interoperability and flexibility to the enterprise.

In Microservices the functional logic is modeled and exposed as software service and is available on demand to other applications. Microservices is recommended cautiously, when the performance is important requirement, functionality is highly available and security is important.

Extensive use of Microservices and "compositional development" by assembling services rather than low-level programming can eventually leave IT with a collection of Microservices and not really a collection of applications.

Microservices are deployable on independent technology stacks. While they leverage Cloud models to deploy and orchestrate Microservices, individual Microservices can still reside on legacy platforms, as per the requirement.

To achieve success with Microservices, enterprises must first build a well-designed application according to existing platform standards; refactor the application into a collection of Microservices as necessary to meet business needs. With the right people, processes, and tools, Microservices can deliver faster development and deployment, easier maintenance, improved scalability, and freedom from long-term technology commitment.

Finally, do not create too many Microservices. Every new Microservice uses multiple resources. Split larger services into Microservices only when the demand is for scaling, lifecycle, or data. Making them too small transfers complexity from the Microservices into the service integration task. Also, avoid sharing Microservices between systems.

It is up to the Enterprise IT architecture team to decided, when to adopt Microservices and when not to go for Microservices based on IT strategy assessment.

2. Service based Architectures

Service-Oriented Architecture (SOA) is an architectural style that supports service-orientation which initially became popular as a way of breaking complex applications down into discrete parts that could be managed easily. SOA is a software development model for distributed application components that incorporate discovery, access control, data mapping and security features. This collection of services that communicate with each other by either data passing or it could involve two or more services coordinating some activity. A third party method of connecting services to each other is often required.

Service based Architectures are generally distributed architectures, where service components be accessed remotely through remote access protocol. Some of the protocols are, Representational State Transfer (REST), Simple Object Access Protocol (SOAP), Advanced Message Queuing Protocol (AMQP), Java Message Service (JMS), Microsoft Message Queuing (MSMQ), Remote Method Invocation (RMI), or .NET Remoting.

Distributed architectures offer significant advantages over monolithic and layered-based architectures, including better scalability, decoupling, and control over development, testing, and deployment. Services within a distributed architecture tend to be more self-contained, allowing for better change control and easier maintenance, which in turn leads to applications that are more robust and more responsive. Main features of the applications built on distributed architectures are loose coupling and modularity.

In the context of service-based architecture, modularity is the practice of encapsulating portions of application into self-contained services that can be individually designed, developed, tested, and deployed with little or no dependency on other components or services in the application.

Section below describes the difference between SOA and Microservices.

2.1 SOA Vs Microservices

Service Oriented Architecture (SOA) is preferred for an enterprise having plenty of legacy systems, heavy weight middleware and diverse applications.

Microservices Architecture is based on SOA vision, which is decomposition of software systems into loosely coupled services. Microservices extends the principles of SOA like business alignment, dependency minimization, and service contracts.

Each Microservice has its own data store, and Centralized or De-centralized governance.

Microservices use continuous integration (CI) and continuous delivery (CD) methodologies and practices, as well as several critical components that were not as common in SOA, such as:

- Polyglot programming and persistence.
- Containers or immutable virtual machines (VMs).

The environment for Microservices architecture is the borderless enterprise, end-to-end, cloud-centric digital applications leveraging virtualized infrastructure.

Below table summarizes difference between SOA and Microservices.

Service Oriented Architecture	Microservice Architecture

SOA started as a conceptual architecture, SOA technologies have evolved from the concepts.	Microservice architecture was derived from real software development patterns observed within numerous organizations
SOA is limited to few aspects of an enterprise such as technology and governance	Microservice architecture is broad, covering the patterns, principles, culture, and enterprise governance and technologies
Built on the concept of a share-as much-as-possible architecture style	Built on share-as-little-as-possible architecture style
SOA was aiming to control and standardize enterprise application integration	Microservices goal is to be as responsive as possible to customer needs while maintaining high levels of software quality and system availability
Focus on standardization at enterprise level and follows the monolithic approach	Allows different applications / teams to evolve autonomously
More complex protocols like BPEL, WS-Choreography are used	Uses representational static transfer (REST) protocol
Loose or decoupled services	Atomicity is main feature of Microservices
In SOA data service layers are implemented using web-services-based data services. The exposed legacy data create-read-update-delete (CRUD) queries as web service operations.	Microservices abstract data services as RESTful resources, where individual Microservices respond to RESTful calls by abstracting underlying CRUD operations.
Replacement of existing applications is complex and requires business case evaluation	Replacement is easy and most cost effective
Based on heavy weight technologies (SOAP, ESB etc) and not highly scalable	Based on lightweight technologies and is very scalable.
Application development and deployment takes longer time and its complex	Application development and deployment is rapid and simple. Less overhead
Centralized Governance. Does not support multiple development teams	Local and distributed governance. Supports multiple development teams working simultaneously and independently
Services need not be independent	Service has to be independent of other service

In summary, both Microservices architecture and SOA are considered service based architectures, meaning that they are architecture patterns that place a heavy emphasis on services as the primary architecture component used to implement and perform business and non-business functionality. Although Microservices and SOA are very different architecture styles, they share many characteristics.

Some defining Characteristics of Microservices are,

- In Microservices architecture, services are small, independent, and loosely coupled
- Each Microservice is a separate codebase, which can be managed by a small development team
- Microservices can be deployed independently. A team can update an existing service without rebuilding and redeploying the entire application
- Microservices are responsible for persisting their own data or external state. This differs from the traditional model, where a separate data layer handles data persistence
- Microservices communicate with each other by using well-defined APIs. Internal implementation details of each service are hidden from other services
- Microservices do not need to share the same technology stack, libraries, or frameworks

The following sections describe the Service characteristics of the Microservices with an example "License Management System" (LMS) used in e-Governance space. The same example is used throughout the book to explain about the designing and development of Microservices based application for the LMS application.

Case Study – License Management System

License and Permits Management System (LMS) is a fictitious License and electronic permit management system to be built using next generation technologies like Microsevices, API first, Cloud deployment. The LMS system serve License and Permits Management across the Government as its core business application. This application aims in managing workflows and maintain database of records related to a variety of permits, trade licenses, periodic inspections and regulatory enforcement programs.

The goal of the LMS application is to provide a next-generation replacement to its current license and permit systems that will provide core tracking and workflow functionalities, as well as to integrate closely with (or replace) other core applications and systems (such as electronic document management, electronic plan review, interactive voice response, electronic payment, geographic information, employee timekeeping, Fees management, reporting) to provide a seamless overall experience for LMS internal and external customers.

The key objective of LMS is to reduce the time for License life cycle processes and to automate online tracking and monitoring of Permits and Licenses. It also covers,

a. To establish a single-window mechanism integrating the services of federal, state and local Governments
b. To reduce the time for License life cycle processes
c. To provide simplified forms, procedures and information in a convenient and cost–effective manner.
d. To enable event-based, online G2B interactions and transactions
e. To enhance transparency, speed, certainty & responsiveness
f. To automate workflow in the respective departments
g. Automated online tracking and monitoring of Permits and Licenses

LMS has various sub domains and processes. The application consists of several components including the LicenseFrontUI, which implements the user interface, along with some backend services for tracking, calculate fee, inspection etc. The application consists of following set of services. The below diagram depicts the sample application of License Management System using Microservices,

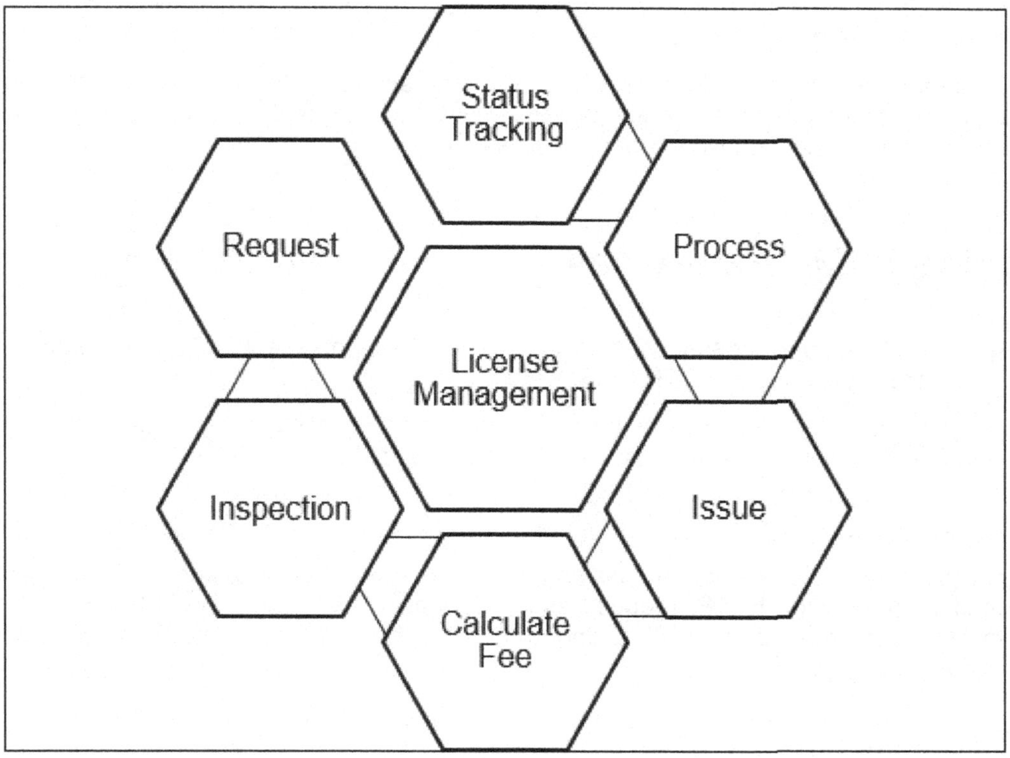

License Management Steps

The To-be LMS application shall address the following,

- Eliminate Manual Processing.
- Remove Usage of Legacy Technologies.
- Better customer experience
- Integrating with other departments for multi-departmental interface services
- Ability to scale to lots of web API calls per day
- Develop and deploy the application in public clouds
- To support multiple channels for citizen and other stakeholder interactions

When the monolithic version is converted to a Microservices version of the LMS application, a web front-end will run with an authentication Microservice on a separate run time. Communication between the Microservices occurs using RESTful calls.

Details of LMS architecture, design, development, patterns used for developing this LMS application are mentioned across the multiple chapters of this book.

2.2 Service Independence

In modern world, the business is highly agile and it changes continuously. This impacts every service and we should be able to manage them. Service independence minimizes the impact to the service infrastructure by identifying and isolating those services that undergo constant churn. Once identified, these services should be upgradeable or replaceable without any additional changes to the software landscape. Since each service is also self-contained, redeployment of each independent service is simplified since there are no service dependencies to manage. Simpler service redeployments streamline release processes since fewer software assets need to be managed from release to release.

A Microservice is independent of other Microservices or other services. Instances of a Microservice are independent of the other instances of the same Microservice. Development and deployment of a Microservice is independent of the development and deployment of other services.

2.3 Messaging in Microservices

In SOA, messaging is mainly through loosely coupled web service level messaging. This is primarily based on SOAP on top of different protocols such as HTTP, JMS.

For Microservices architecture, it is required to have a simple and lightweight messaging mechanism. The following are the 3 ways of messaging popularly used in Microservices architecture.

Synchronous Messaging

REST is the best choice for synchronous messaging in Microservices Architecture. It provides a simple messaging style implemented with HTTP request-response, based on resource API style. Most of the Microservices implementations are using HTTP along with resource API based styles as an alternative to REST/HTTP synchronous messaging.

Asynchronous Messaging

In a Microservices scenario, where the client does not expect the response immediately or does not accept the response at all, it is required to use asynchronous messaging techniques. In such scenarios, asynchronous messaging protocols such as AMQP, STOMP, or MQTT are widely used.

Message Formats

In most of the Microservices-based applications, simple text-based message formats such as JSON and XML are used on top of HTTP resource API style.

2.4 Service Contracts

A service contract is an agreement between remote service and the client that specifies the inbound and outbound data. The general contract format is, XML, JavaScript Object Notation, Java object etc.

There exist two basic types of service contracts in service-based architecture,

- Service-based contracts
- Consumer-driven contracts

Service-based contracts

The service is the sole owner of the contract and is generally free to evolve and change the contract without considering the needs of the service consumers. This model forces all service consumers to adopt new service contract changes, whether or not the service consumers need or want the new service functionality.

Consumer-driven contracts

These are based on a closer relationship between the service and the service consumers. With this model there is strong collaboration between the service owner and the service consumers so that needs of the service consumers are taken into account with respect to the contracts that bind them. This type of model generally requires the service to know who its consumers are and how the service is used by each service consumer.

Contract versioning allows an enterprise to roll out new service features that involve contract changes and at the same time provide backward compatibility for service consumers that are still using prior contracts.

Below figure shows that the contract used by service consumer (Fee Service) and service consumer (Inspection Service) are both the same circle shape (signifying the same contract) but contain different version numbers.

A simple example of this might be an XML based contract that represents an order for some goods, with a contract version number 1.0.

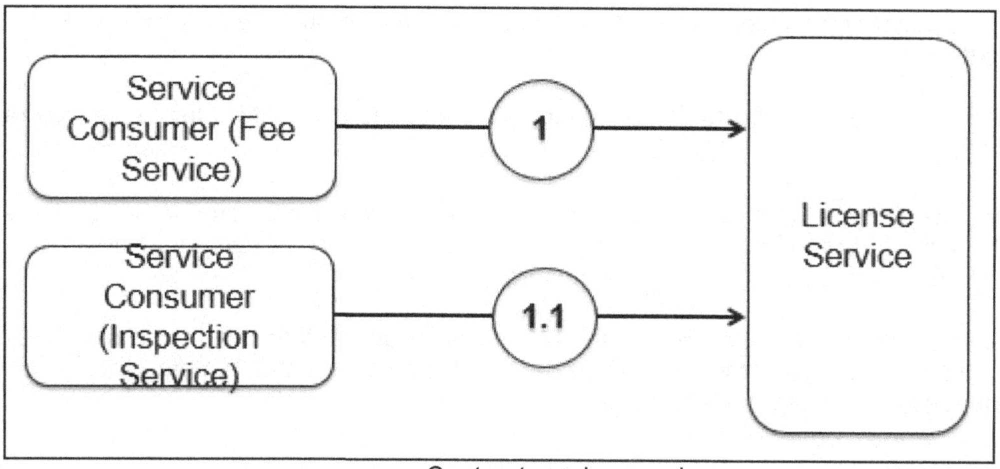

Contract version numbers

In the above diagram, the contract used by service consumer (Fee Service) and service consumer (Inspection Service) are both the same circle shape indicating the same contract but contain different version numbers. As an example, an XML based contract that represents an order for some service to customer, with a contract version number 1.0. A newer version (version 1.1) is released containing an additional field used to provide delivery instructions in the event the recipient is not available at the time of delivery. In this case the original contract (version 1.0) can remain backward compatible by making the new delivery instructions field optional.

2.5 Service Availability

Service availability is the ability of a remote service to accept requests in a timely manner. Service responsiveness is the ability of the service consumer to receive a timely response from the service. The diagram below depicts the service availability and service responsiveness.

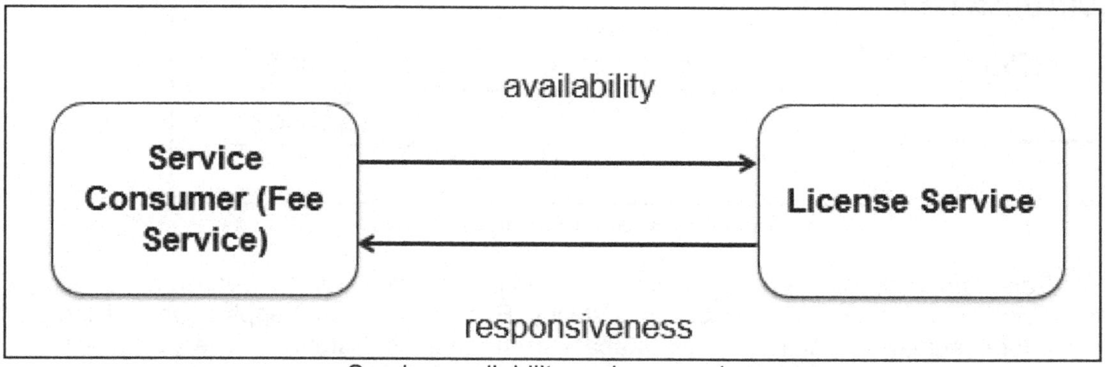

Service availability and responsiveness

Service availability is related to service connectivity, there is not much a service consumer can do except to retry the connection for a set number of times or queue the request for later processing if possible.

Service responsiveness is much more difficult to address. The questions is once a request is sent to a service, how long should the consumer wait for a response. The possibility is the service is just slow, or something happened in the service to prevent the response.

2.6 Security

Service consumer need to be both authenticated and authorized to access a particular service.

Authentication, service consumer can connect to the service, usually through sign-on credentials using a username and password.

Authorization, service consumer is allowed to access specific business functionality within a service based on entitlement (usually the role).

With Microservices, security becomes a challenge primarily because no middleware component handles security-based functionality. There are two models, each service must handle security on its own, or API/Gateway layer to be made more intelligent to handle the security aspects of the application.

Although this design can be modified to delegate both authentication and authorization to a separate security service, encapsulating the authorization in the service itself to avoid chattiness with a remote security service and to create a stronger bounded context with fewer external dependencies.

2.7 Service Transactions

Given that service-based architectures are generally distributed architectures, it is extremely difficult to propagate and maintain a transaction context across multiple remote services.

As illustrated in Figure below, a single service request calls multiple remote services to complete the request.

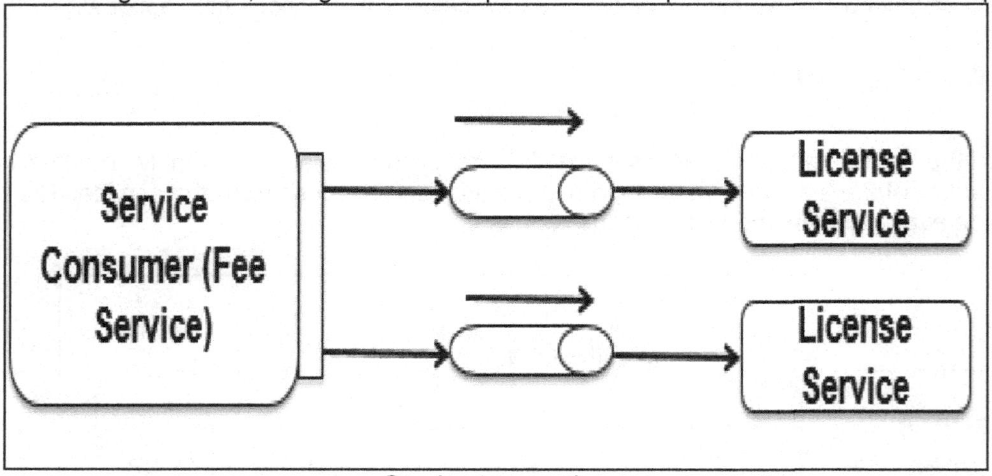

Service transaction management

In Microservices Paradigm, a single business service is fulfilled by multiple services. Service based architectures relay on basic availability, soft state and eventual consistency (BASE). Distributed applications relying on these transactions strive for eventual consistency in the database rather than consistency at every transaction.

As an example of BASE transactions is making a Payment for License Renewal at the one of the delivery centres. When we make the payment at these delivery centres, it can take from several minutes to several hours for the payment to appear in our account. In other words, there is a soft transition state in which the money has left our hands but has not reached concerned license department account. We are tolerant of this time lag and rely on soft state and eventual consistency, knowing and trusting that the money will reach concerned department at some point soon. Batch jobs also sometimes rely on eventual consistency when seen from a holistic system view.

2.8 Service Taxonomy

Classification of Services within the Microservices Architecture is termed as Service Taxonomy. Service Classification are of two types, Business Service Type and Business Area. Business Service type is the type of role the service plays in the overall architecture.

For example, some business services might implement business functionality like License Management, whereas other services might implement some sort of non-business functionality such as logging, auditing, and security.

Business area is the role of business service plays with regard to a specific business functional area such as reporting, license processing and License delivery.

Microservices architectures have a limited service taxonomy when it comes to service type classification, mostly consisting of only two service types as shown in the diagram below.

- Functional services are services that support specific business operations or functions. Functional services are accessed externally and are generally not shared with any other service.
- Infrastructure services support non-functional tasks such as authentication, authorization, auditing, logging, and monitoring. Infrastructure services are not exposed to the outside world but rather are treated as private shared services only available internally to other services.

In Microservices architecture, these are services that implement nonfunctional tasks such as auditing, security, and logging.

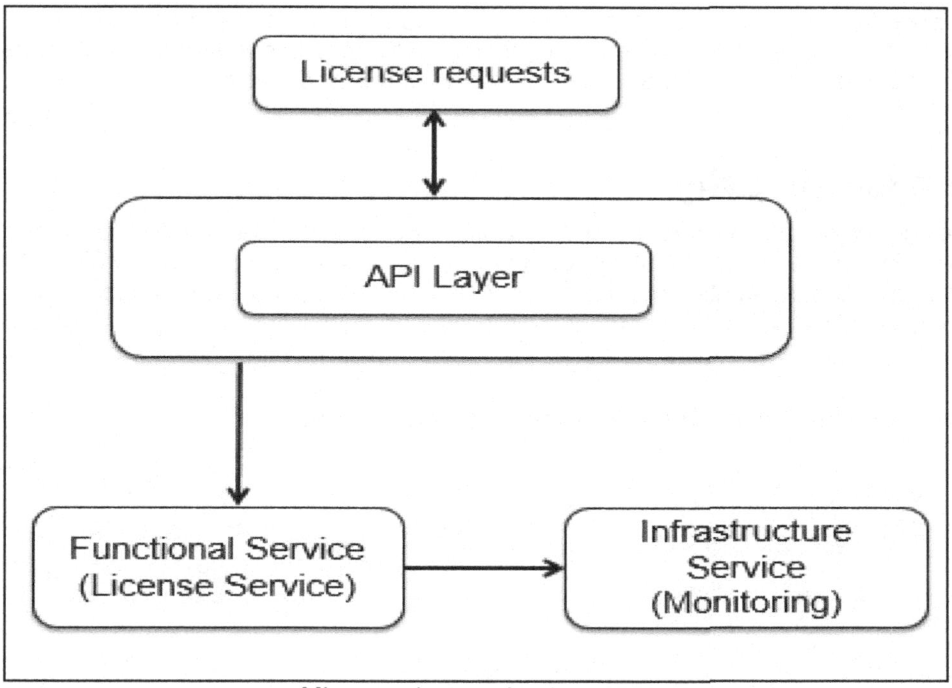

Microservice service taxonomy

2.9 Service Ownership and Coordination

Service owner is the type of group within the organization that is responsible for creating and maintaining a service. In Microservices architecture the application development teams own both the infrastructure and functional services.

Figure below illustrates the typical service ownership model for Microservices.

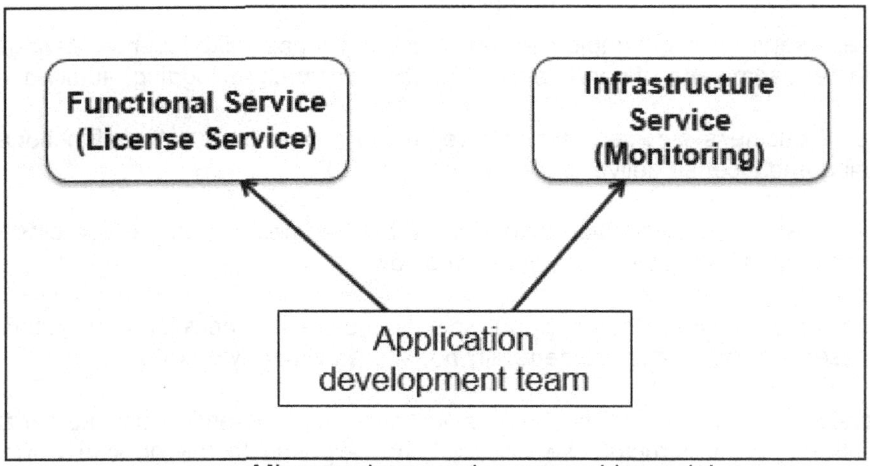

Microservices service ownership model

With Microservices, there is little or no coordination among services to fulfill a single business request. If coordination is needed among service owners, it is done quickly and efficiently through small application development teams.

In Microservices very minimal coordination is needed among the application development teams. These services are developed and tested quickly and deployed through an effective deployment model. This leads to faster time to market, lower development and maintenance costs, and more robust applications.

2.10 Service Granularity

Microservices are generally small, fine-grained services. More specifically, service components within a Microservices architecture are generally single-purpose services that do one thing well. Service granularity affects both performance and transaction management. Services that are too fine-grained will require inter service communication to fulfill a single business request, resulting in numerous remote service calls that take up valuable time.

The diagram below shows the Service Granularity impact on transactions.

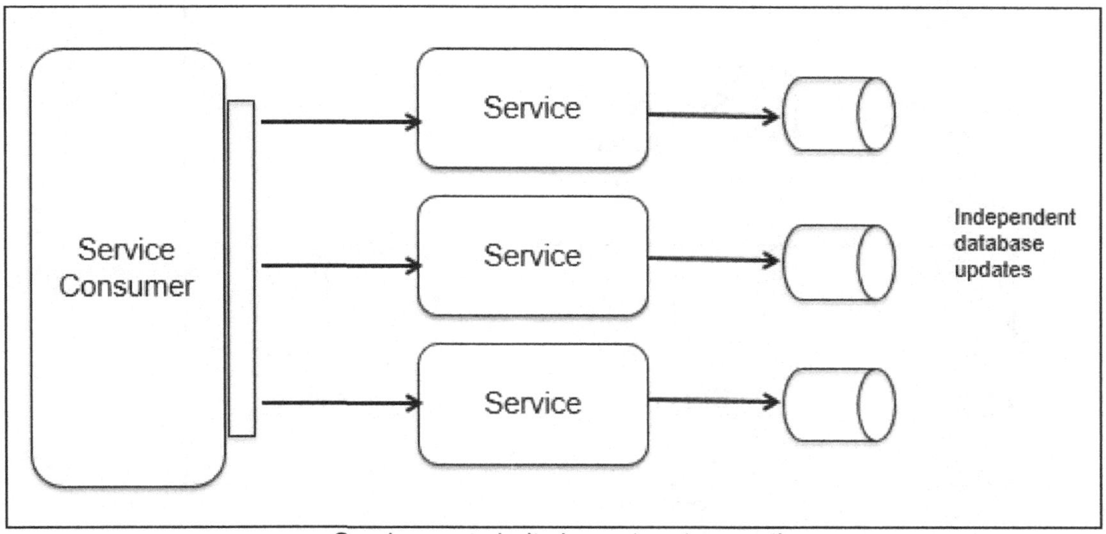

Service granularity impact on transactions

Microservices can be declared with varying levels of capability and the size of the functionality is typically referred to as its granularity. Since Microservices are discrete and must be composed into greater functional entities to support business processes, it follows that message passing between Microservices increases as the Microservices become finer-grained.

Achieving an optimum level of granularity is therefore of interest to application developers and the key factors that contribute to this can be summarized as follows:

Business Need: The needs of a business may be changing rapidly and demanding new functionality from an application. This growth may not be manageable within the existing application architecture and therefore a granular approach is adopted. It is typical for application developers to use the functionality itself to set the scope that determines the size of a Microservice

Size of application: For smaller applications the level of granularity could be fine-grained. For enterprise (larger) sized applications, the granularity is likely to be at a higher level (coarser) with each Microservice built up from smaller Microservices. However, for smaller applications there may still need to be an aggregation of services to facilitate simpler communication and reduced latency over IoT network connections

Database design: The design of a database may have an impact on granularity. For example, in a retail scenario if there is a product service and an order service, the functional decomposition is likely to have led to the implementation of separate data repositories for each service. Any association of the data between the databases will be implemented at code level, leading to more coarse-grained Microservices.

Reuse: MSA promotion of reuse in the architecture is a concern for enterprise applications. If the services are fine grained, then reuse is possible but there is the additional overhead of wiring the services together. If the services are too coarse grained, then it is difficult to reuse the services.

2.11 Service Orchestration and Choreography

The term service orchestration refers to the coordination of multiple services through a centralized mediator such as a service consumer or an integration hub. Some of the examples of Integration hubs are Mule, Camel, Spring Integration etc.

The diagram below illustrates the concept of service orchestration.

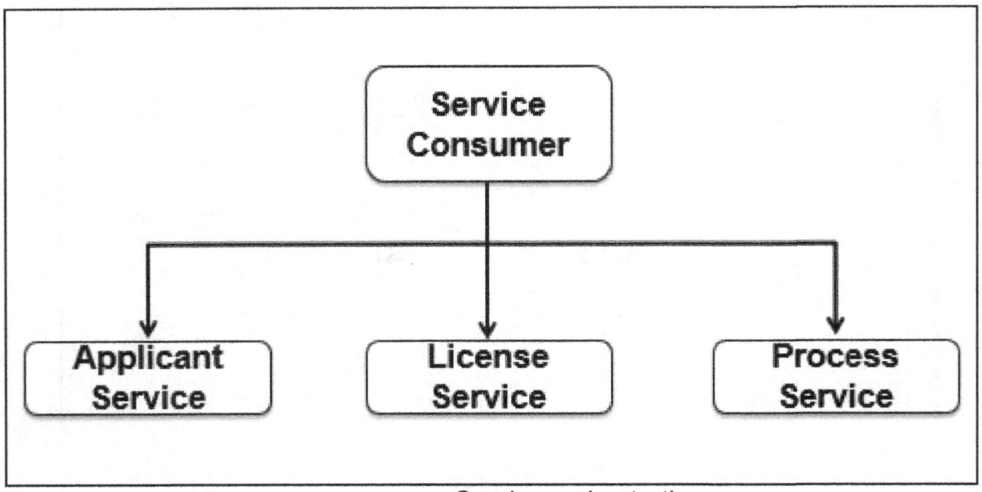

Service orchestration

Service choreography refers to the coordination of multiple service calls without a central mediator. The term inter-service communication is sometimes used in conjunction with service choreography.

With service choreography, one service calls another service, which may call another service and so on, performing what is also referred to as service chaining. This concept is illustrated in below diagram.

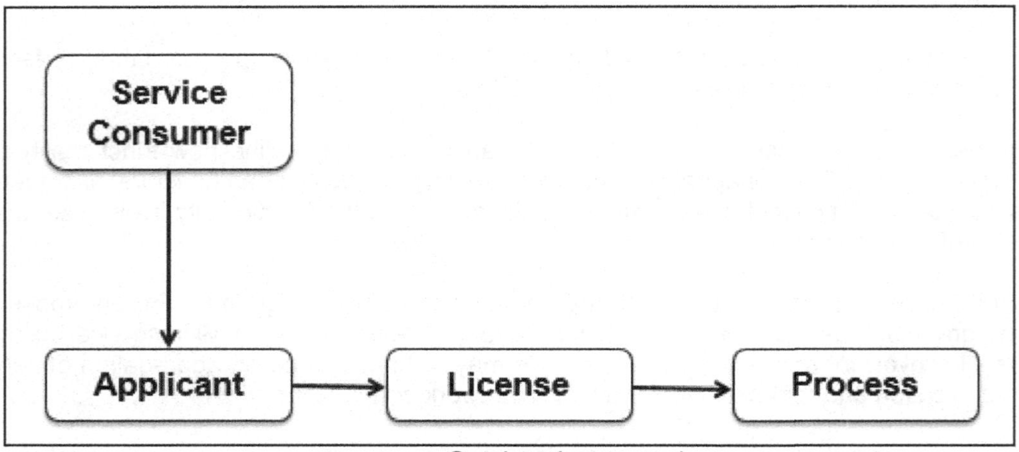

Service choreography

Microservices architecture favors service choreography over service orchestration, primarily because the architecture topology lacks a centralized middleware component. The diagram below shows that the overall architecture topology consists of only two major components, service components and an API layer.

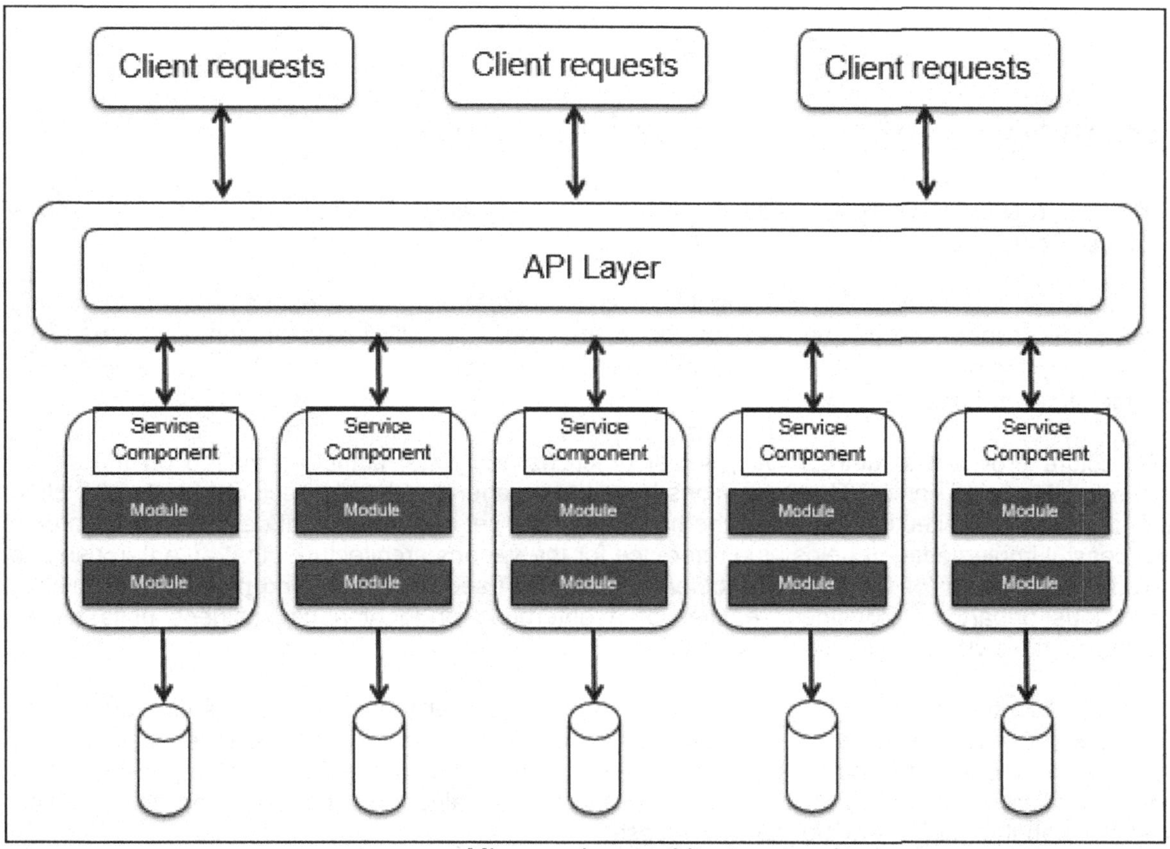

Microservices architecture topology

Because Microservices architecture is a share-as-little-as-possible architecture, minimize the amount of service choreography in the architecture, restricting interactions to those between functional services and infrastructure services.

2.12 Summary

In this chapter, we have highlighted the difference between two types of service based architectures SOA and Microservices with respect to characteristics and patterns.

In summary, Microservices and SOA both rely on services as the main architecture component; they vary greatly in terms of service characteristics. The chapter also covers the comparison of Microservices and SOA by focusing on how the services are classified within each pattern (i.e., service taxonomy), how services are coordinated based on the service owner, and finally the difference in service granularity between Microservices and SOA.

Also, it provides the global view of architectural aspects, including the level of sharing among components, service orchestration and choreography, the use of middleware vs. a simple API layer, and finally differences in how remote services are accessed in each pattern.

3. Microservices Reference Architecture

For enterprises, moving to Microservices is a seismic shift in web application development and delivery and is crucial for the success of customers today.

There exist many different approaches for defining Microservices Reference Architecture and implementing Microservices, and many of them are unique and specific to the needs of individual development teams. This demands a need for designing reference models to develop and deliver Microservices-based applications that are consumed across the Organizations.

A Reference Architecture provides a methodology, set of practices, template, standards based on the set of successful solutions implemented earlier. These solutions have been generalized and structured for the depiction of both a logical and physical architecture based on the harvesting of a set of patterns that describe observations in a number of successful implements. It helps as a reference for the various architectures that an enterprise can implement to provide the solution for the various problems. It can be used as the starting point or the point of comparisons for various departments/Business entities of a enterprise or for various business units for an enterprise. It provides multiple views for multiple stakeholders.

Today, enterprises are adopting technologies like analytics, mobility, social media, IoT and smart embedded devices to change customer relationships, internal processes and value propositions. Microservices acts as building blocks for building modern distributed enterprise systems and become one of the enablers in the digital transformation journey. Microservices provides the agility, reliability, maintainability, scalability and deploy ability that aid enterprises through their digital transformation process.

There exists, numerous articles and blogs on Microservices reference architecture, architecture principles and best practices. The following sections of this chapter summarizes the authors view of the purpose of Microservices Reference Architecture, drivers for adopting Microservices, architecture principles and logical view of Microservices Reference Architecture.

3.1 Purpose of Microservices Reference Architecture

In most of the cases, architects spend lot of time researching, investigating, defining and re-arguing architectural decisions. It is like reinventing the wheel as their peers in other organizations or even the same organization have already spent lot of time and effort defining their own architectural practices. This prevents the Organization from learning from its own experiences and applying that knowledge for increased effectiveness.

Reference architecture provides missing architectural information that can be provided in advance to project team members to enable consistent architectural best practices.

Reference Architecture helps an Enterprise to achieve the following at the abstract level,

- Reference architecture is more of communication channel to an enterprise
- Helps the Business Owners to accommodate their strategies, vision, objectives and principles
- Evaluating the IT systems based on Reference Architecture Principles
- Reduction in the IT spending in terms of increasing functionality, availability and scalability etc
- Real time Integration Model, helps to reduce the latency of the data updates
- Used to define single source of Information
- Provides the clear vision on the managing of the information and security
- Define the policy around the data ownership, Product boundaries etc
- Cost Optimization across Project and Solution Portfolios, by eliminating unused or duplicate investments and assets
- Shorter Implementation Time and Cost

One of the biggest changes in application design and architecture when moving to Microservices is using the network to communicate between functional components of the application. In monolithic apps, application components communicate in memory. In Microservices application, that communication happens over the network, so network design and implementation become critically important.

Microservices Reference Architecture is:

- To provide customers and the industry with ready-to-use blueprints for building Microservices-based systems, speeding – and improving – development
- To create a platform for testing new features, whether developed internally or externally
- To help understand partner systems and components so we can gain a holistic perspective on the Microservices ecosystem

Once the reference architecture is in place, the set of architectural principles, standards, reference models, and best practices ensure that the aligned investments have the greatest possible likelihood of success in both the near term and the long term (TCO).

3.2 Common Pitfalls of Microservices Adoption

Microservices reference architecture serves as the first step towards maturity for the industry adoption. During the course of our assignments/experiences with industry players, we have come across the following observations - some of these indicate a lack of maturity of the Microservices adoption:

- Most of the organizations do not have a clue on where to start the Microsevices adoption
- No clue on the capabilities that enterprises need to start adopting Microservices architecture style at scale
- Organizations have a minimum knowledge on the Technologies usage to ensure successful adoption to get best of Microservices architecture. Microservices is largely centered around new-age development practices like DevOps, APIs, Containers and Cloud Infrastructure.
- There are no proven enterprise adoption patterns, as there is very little enterprise wide adoption outside Internet native companies.
- Choice of Polyglot, the freedom with which developers can independently develop and deploy services is reliant on the choice of architecture. A wrong choice of architecture will also restrict the smoothness with which each service can communicate with each other

3.3 Drivers for Microservices Reference Architecture

Microservices are smaller in scope, which is determined by a focus on domain boundaries and consistent domain modeling, and require less code. Deployment strategies including focused, self-contained archives—often packaged as Linux containers and CI/CD—lead to faster, more reliable deployments. As a result, the software development lifecycle becomes faster in general.

With Microservices, each service can scale independently to meet temporary or seasonal traffic increases, complete batch processing, and meet other business needs. Improved fault isolation restricts service issues, such as memory leaks or open database connections, to only affect that specific service. The scalability of Microservices complements the flexibility of cloud services, letting an enterprise improve service while also handling more customers simultaneously without interrupting service.

Below diagram represents few key drivers for enterprises adopting Microservices.

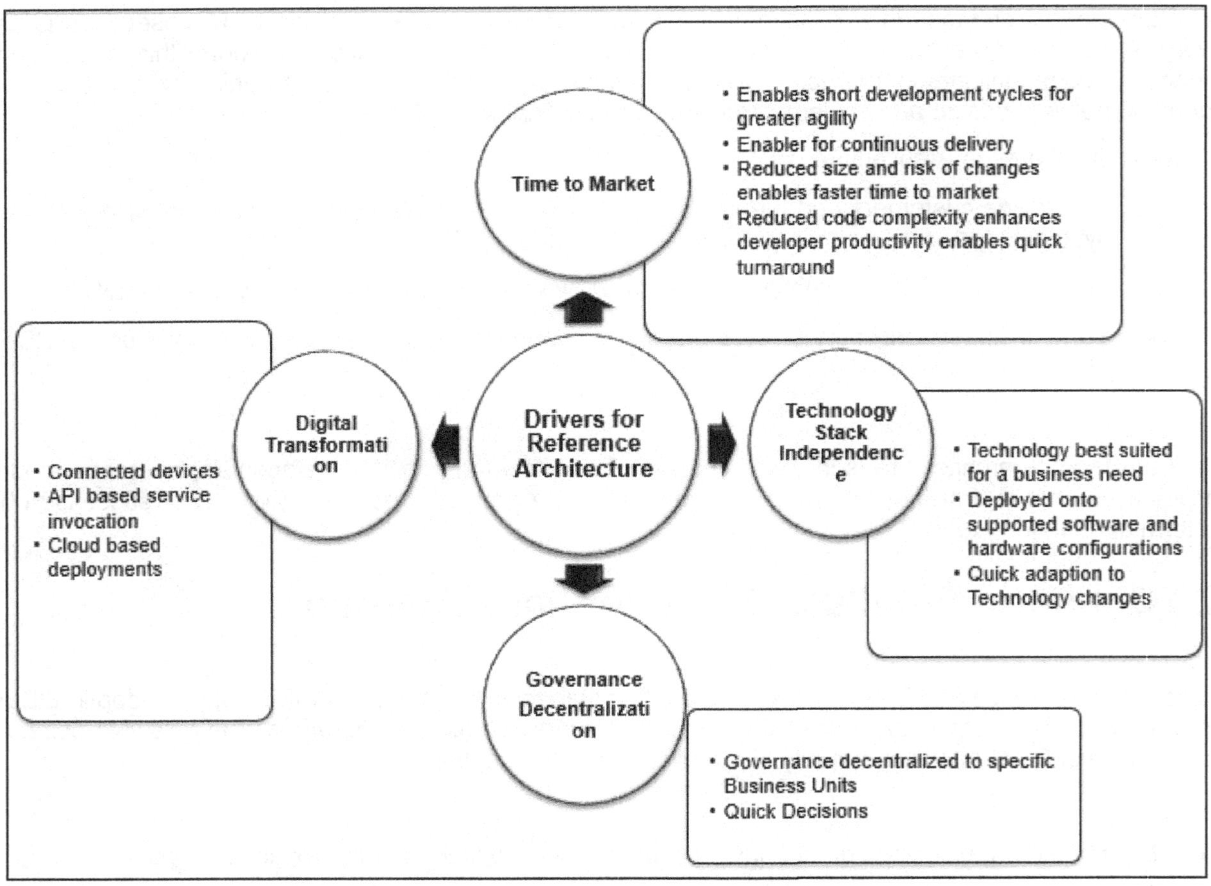

Drivers for Microservices Reference Architecture

3.4 Microservices Architecture Principles

Every architecture is formed based on certain design principles and Microservices is no different. This chapter will not talk about what Microservices is all about. There are already plenty of articles and blogs to do that. In this chapter, the author's talk about what it takes to devise a Microservices based architecture. We will take a look at some of the design principles one should take into account to design a Microservices based applications.

The services in the Reference Architecture are designed to be lightweight, ephemeral and stateless. Below are few key architectural principles for Microservices:

Single Responsibility Principle: Single responsibility, defined by MSA, is the direct alignment of a service to a singular business activity. For the purpose of this discussion, a business activity can be described as a unit of work performed by the organization that supports an existing business process or function. For single responsibility, the obligation of the service is to map completely to the business activity and deliver whatever business logic is necessary to fulfill the activity. Having each service associated with a single business activity enables the tracking of business change impact through the software service landscape. Impacted services can be more readily and easily identified when supporting a single business responsibility.

It is important to decompose the target business process to the right level to achieve the single responsibility, aligned to an atomic business activity, as well as to achieve the decoupled nature to support the resilience and scalability of the solution.

The decomposition can be guided by the scale cube and its three dimensions of scaling, particularly the y-axis scaling, which emphasizes the functional decomposition through splitting of applications into multiple Microservices.

The other influencing concept is the bounded context from DDD, which can help determine the right level of decomposition through context mapping.

Granular: Microservice granularity is contained within the intersection of a single functional domain, a single data domain and its immediate dependencies, a self-sufficient packaging and a technology domain. Self-containment dictates that a service shall encompass all external IT resources (e.g., data sources, business rules) necessary to support the business activity. In addition, self-containment necessitates that service dependencies falling outside the scope of the development team should be minimized or preferably eliminated. By adhering to self-containment, services are inherently more easily replaceable and upgradeable. Along with single responsibility, this characteristic also promotes single ownership of the service since it encapsulates not only specific business requirements (single responsibility) but also specific software dependencies (self-containment).

Microservices are packaged with containers and components as single-deployment units.

The self-containment principle does not remove the need for orchestration between Microservices. The orchestration function is moved to the application and user interaction layer. Hence, to achieve self-containment, proper granularity in decomposition is essential.

Highly Resilient: An MSA must be a highly-resilient architecture. Its Microservices must be designed for potential failures because individual service failures should not impinge negatively on the user experience. Since a Microservice represents a single responsibility and is self-contained, a service failure could mean that a given business function or process is unable to complete successfully. Lengthy service downtime could also have a significant impact on the entire business. Thus, mechanisms must be in place to ensure timely service recovery. Real-time service monitoring can provide a proactive means for identifying services that are struggling under heavy load or unable to satisfy existing Service-Level Agreements (SLAs). Real-time monitoring of business metrics also provides insight to future business activity changes that will ripple down to IT services. Further, because of the independence of the underlying Microservice, new instantiations will be automatically deployed immediately to allow for business continuity without the resolution of the failure itself.

Domain Driven Design: Domain driven design is an architectural principle in-line with object-oriented approach. It considers the business domain, elements and behaviors and interactions between business domains.

Encapsulation: Each Microservice encapsulates the internal implementation details, so that the external system utilizes the services need not worry about the internals. Encapsulation reduces the complexity and enhances the flexibility of the system.

Loose Coupling: There must be zero coordination necessary for the deployment with other Microservices. The changes in one microsystem should have zero or minimum impact on other services in the eco-system.

In order to maintain minimal service dependencies, Microservices must be highly decoupled. To achieve this decoupling, the business function must be capable of being decomposed down to the level where a Microservice is implementing a single atomic business function. It is this decomposition, and the consequent removal of dependencies between the atomic business functions, that permits the service independence and self-containment required in an MSA.

By relying heavily on existing protocols whose sole purpose is to route messages (HTTP, for example), the needs of a service can be reduced to receiving the message request, applying the appropriate business logic, and generating a message response. MSA discourages the use of external data transformation or protocol bridging services since they introduce additional tightly-coupled service dependencies that will need to be managed during upgrades. MSA endorses the concept of smart endpoints, where all logic needed to manage the incoming request and produce an appropriate response remains encapsulated within the service

Isolation: Services must be designed to work in isolation. When a monolithic system is broken into set of services, it is necessary that these services are decoupled from one another, are made more cohesive and self-sufficient. Each service should be able to handle its failure without breaking the whole application or system. Isolating and decoupling enables service to recover itself from the failure condition very quickly. The isolation characteristic of the service has the following benefits: easy adoption of continuous delivery, better scaling, effective monitoring and testability.

Autonomous: Isolation paves the way for autonomy. Services must be designed to be autonomous. It must be cohesive and able to fulfill its function independently. Every service can be independently invoked using a well-defined API (URI). The API in a way identifies the service function. Autonomous service must also deal with its own data. More popular term is polyglot persistence where each service has its own persistence store. Autonomy also ensures resiliency. An autonomous service has the following benefits: Effective service orchestration and coordination, better scaling, communication through well-defined API, faster and controlled deployment

Asynchronous Communication: While drawing discrete boundaries and designing services with its own bounded context, it is necessary that service communication across boundaries must be asynchronous. The asynchronous mode of communication naturally leads to loose coupling between services and allows for better scaling. With synchronous communication, a call is blocked and waiting for the response. A service in a blocking state cannot perform another task until the response is received and the underlying thread is released. It leads to network congestion and impacts both latency and throughput. Asynchronous communication can also bring in the notion of implementing a well-defined integration or communication pattern to achieve a logical workflow involving different services

Separation of Concerns: Develop the Microservices based on distinct features with zero overlap with other functions. The main objective is to reduce the interaction between services so that they are highly cohesive and loosely coupled. If we separate, the functionality across wrong boundaries will lead tight coupling and increased complexity between services.

Language Neutral: Microservices are composed together to form a complex application, and they do not need to be written using the same programming language. For example, Java might be the correct language for one application, and in others, it might be Python etc

Hexagonal Architecture: This allows an application to equally driven by users, programs, automated test or batch scripts, to be developed and tested in isolation from its eventual run-time devices and databases. Microservice exposes RESTful APIs for external communication; message broker interface for event notification and database adapters for persistence makes hexagonal architecture as a most suitable style for Microservice development.

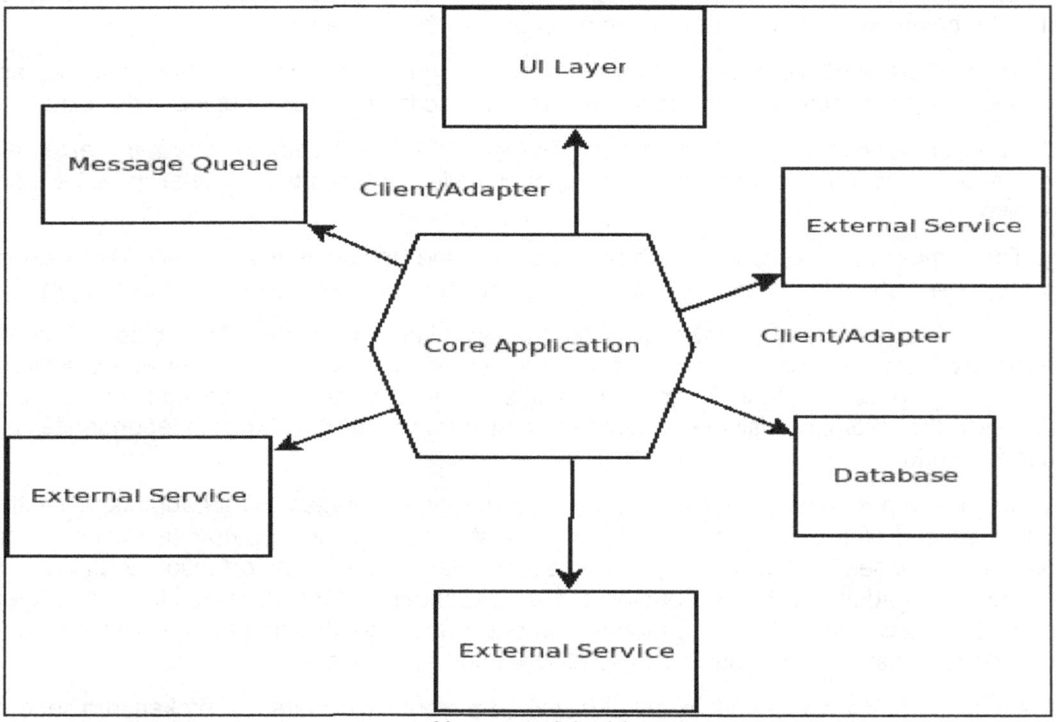

Hexagonal Architecture

3.5 Enterprise Capabilities Leveraged

- Dynamic Service Registry Microservice registers itself with a Service Registry when up.
- Log Aggregation The logs generated by Microservice can be aggregated for central analysis and troubleshooting

- External Configuration the Microservice can get the parameters and properties from an external Configuration like Consul Provisioning & Auto scaling The service is automatically started by a PAAS environment if it detects a need to start additional Instance
- API Gateway A Microservice interface can be exposed to the clients or other divisions via an API gateway that provides Abstraction, Security, Throttling, Service Aggregation

3.6 Microservices Reference Architecture

Microservices is an architecture style, in which software systems or applications are composed of one or more independent and self-contained services. It is not a product, framework, or platform. It is a strategy for building large distributed systems. Microservices are loosely coupled and deployed independently of one another.

Currently, any technology can be used to create a Microservice, if it exposes JavaScript Object Notation (JSON) or Extensible Markup Language (XML) over the HTTP to provide a REST API. These standards would provide guidelines about how to describe, maintain, and retire Microservices.

This architecture style is used when,

- Large applications that require a high release velocity
- Complex applications that need to be highly scalable
- Applications with rich domains or many subdomains
- An organization that consists of small development teams

Below is the logical view of the Microservices reference architecture

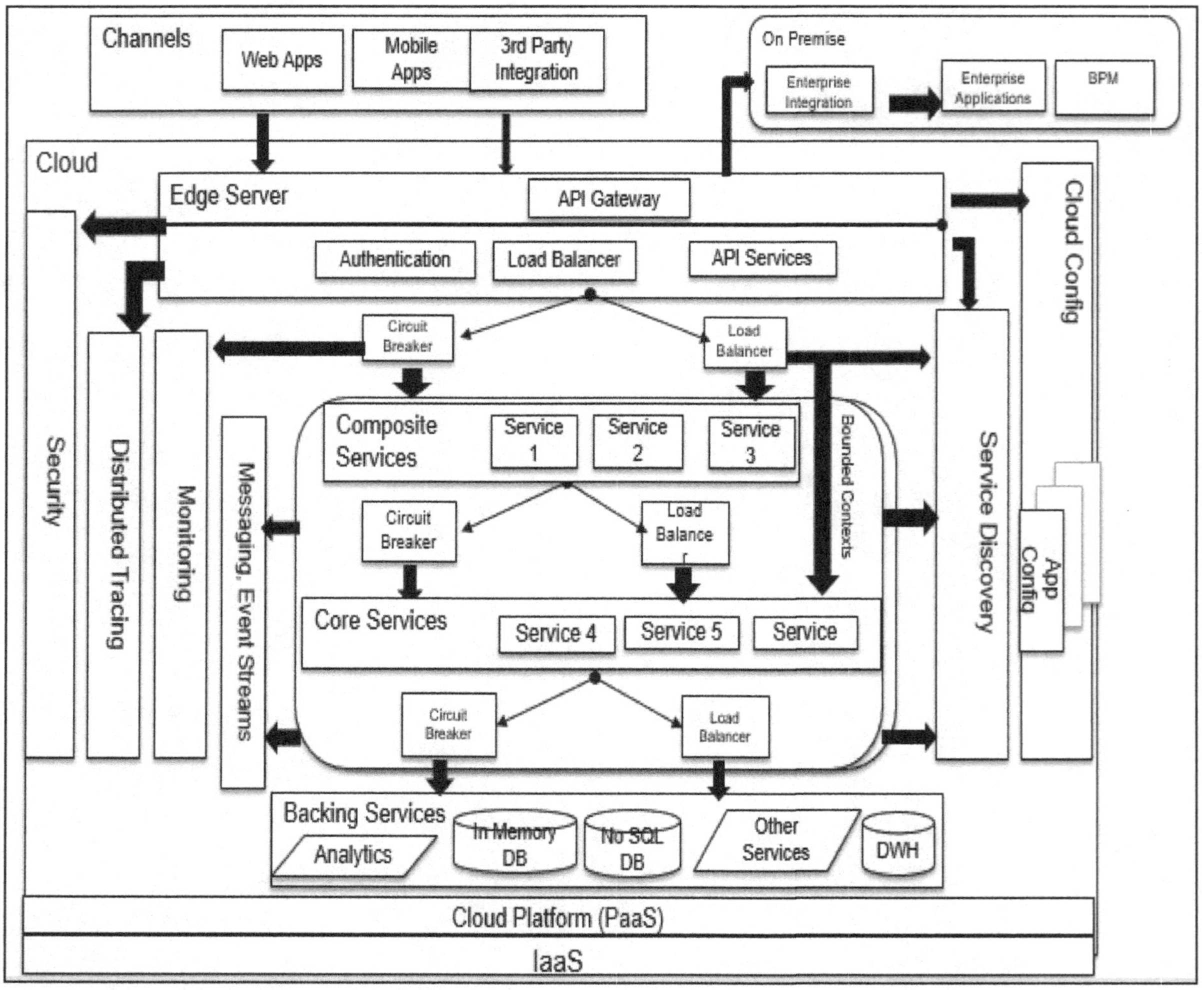

Microservices Reference Architecture - Logical View

Below section briefly describes about various components for the reference architecture:

Channels: Channels represents various client side or consumer applications, which will interact with Microservices.

Edge Server: API services or edge services reside on edge server or the API Gateway. Channels interact with the edge services, which decouples the Microservices, and keep them channel agnostic.

API gateway: is the single entry point for all clients. API Gateway is responsible for aggregating data or, in some cases, acting as a simple routing layer for appropriate services. The API gateway can be seen as a single point of failure. A better approach may be to create multiple API gateways for the different platform or frontends that applications need to support. API Gateway can also be used to coordinate between cloud and on premise communication.

The API gateway helps in:

- Decouple clients from services. Services can be versioned or refactored without needing to update all of the clients
- Services can use messaging protocols that are not web friendly, such as AMQP
- The API Gateway can perform other cross-cutting functions such as authentication, logging, SSL termination, and load balancing

Load Balancer: Microservices applications require load balancing to an even greater degree than monolithic applications. The architecture of a Microservices application relies on multiple, small services working in concert to provide application functionality. This inherently requires robust, intelligent load balancing, especially where external clients access the service APIs directly. Load balancer is software based load balancing used for communication between Microservices and typically be configured for each service for availability and scalability. This restricts the impact of the failure of a single Microservice instance and maintains overall system reliability. Below diagram show load-balancing scheme.

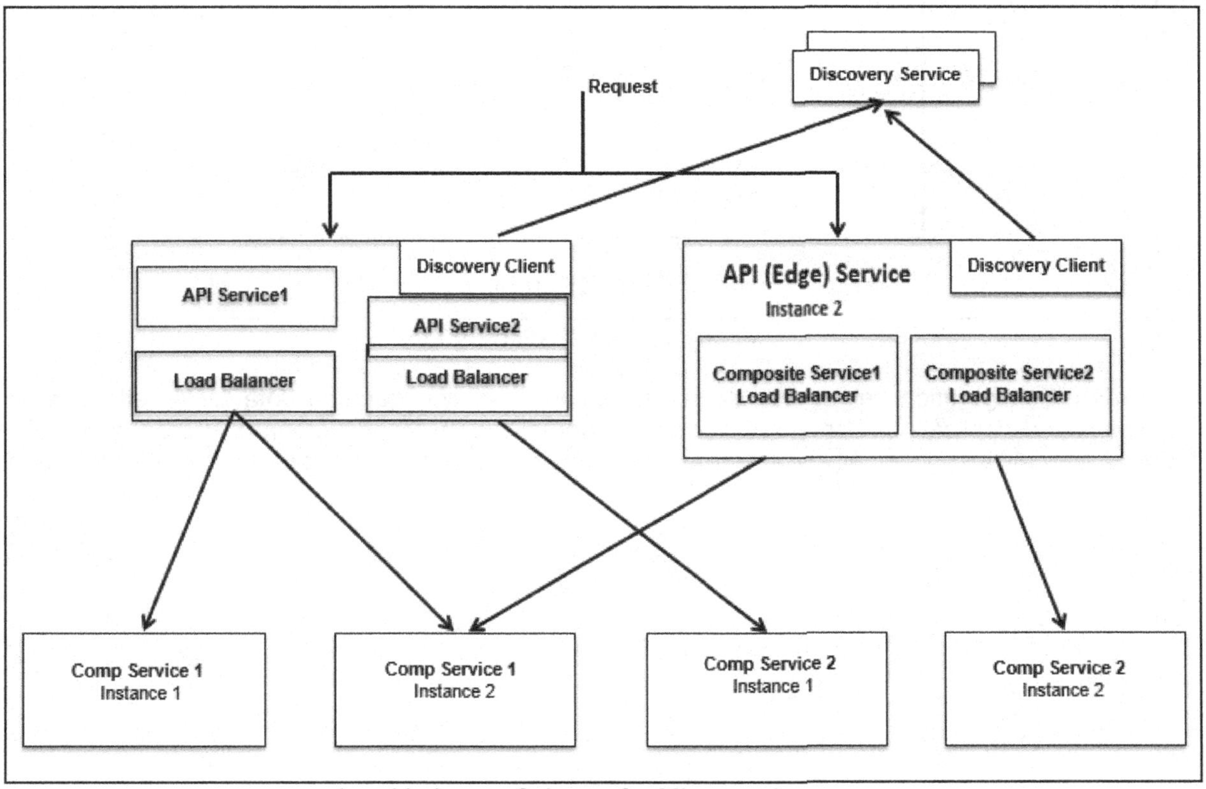

Load balancer Scheme for Microservices

API Service: API services are exposed either on the edge server or on API Gateway. They expose client specific API and can also act as coarse-grained services to orchestrate across multiple Microservices within or across bounded contexts. These services can interact with composite services or directly with core services. API services can also communicate with the enterprise integration infrastructure (typically ESB/MOM) to access any enterprise application on premise

Composite Service: Composite services orchestrate across multiple core services. These services will be communicating with the other services using the event-sourcing model or other means like orchestration.

Core services: These services are the basic building blocks for Microservices architecture. These services encapsulate an entity or an aggregate (fine grained) within a given bounded context. Best practice says that the granularity of the Microservices should be fine grained.

Circuit Breaker: Fault tolerance will ensure that when there is failure happened, failed services does not adversely affect the entire system. Without proper mechanisms in place, errors, in particular, latencies will trickle up to the calling clients where they will potentially exhaust limited resources. When cascading failures occur, the overall system availability is significantly affected.

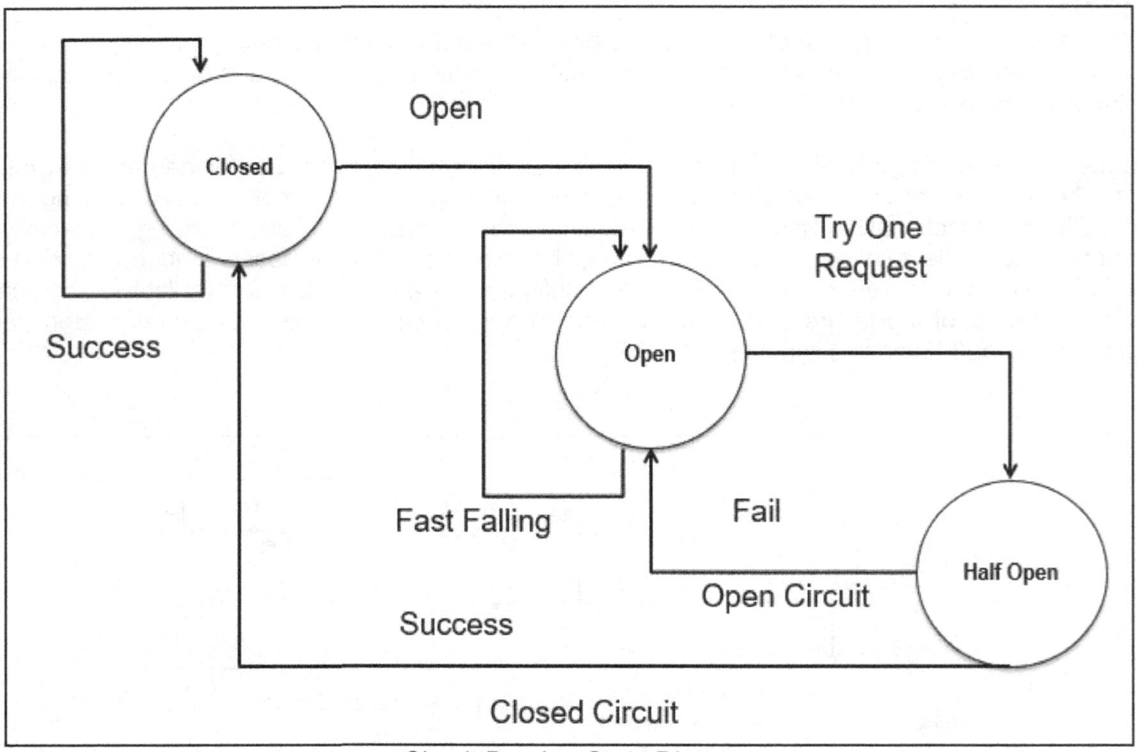

Circuit Breaker State Diagram

Cloud Config: Configuration server acts as a single source of configuration data for all other services in a Microservice-based application. Configuration server externalizes the configuration of a project into an external repository. Each Microservice will connect to configuration server on startup to get the values for their configuration.

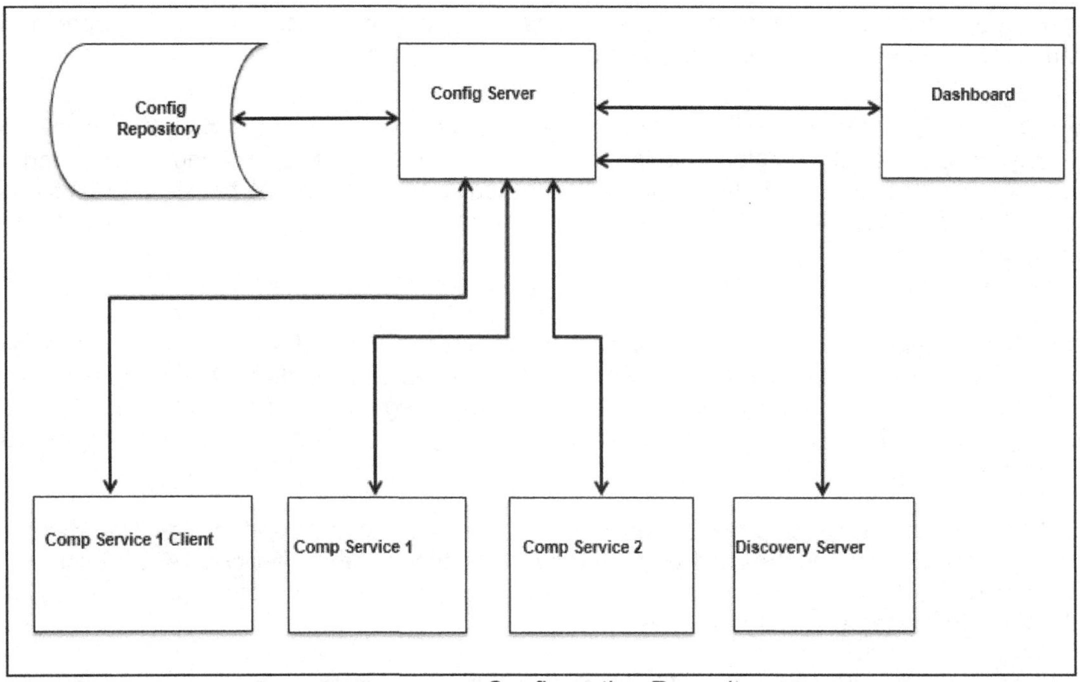

Configuration Repository

Service Discovery: In a modern, cloud-based Microservices application, service instances will be dynamically assigned network locations. Moreover, the set of service instances changes dynamically because of auto-scaling, failures, and upgrades. Consequently, client code needs to use a service discovery mechanism.

Messaging & Events Stream: Lightweight messaging platforms like AMQP will be used for exchange of messages between Microservice within or across bounded contexts or in case of event sourcing used as part of the choreography. Messaging will also be used Microservices to put diagnostics and metrics for the intended for use by monitoring infrastructure.

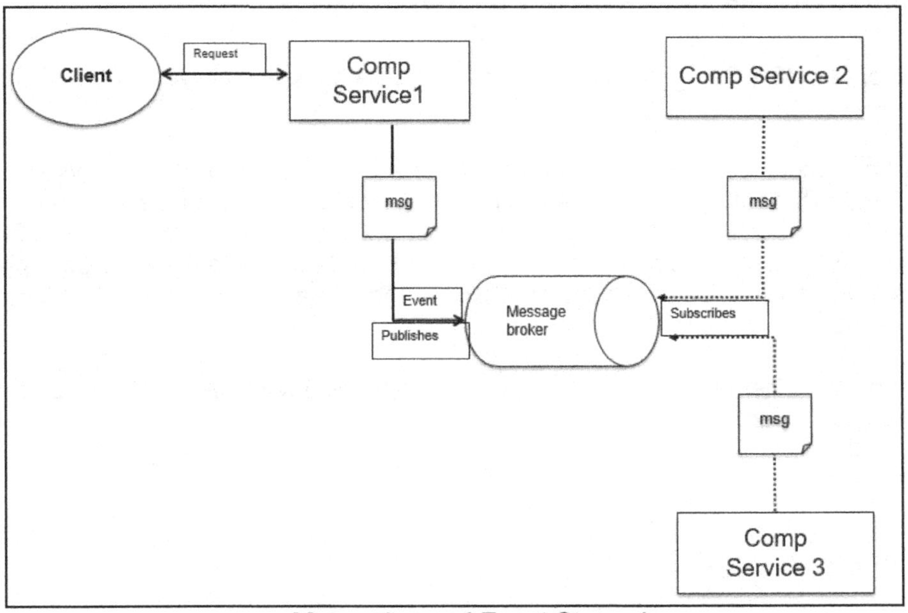

Messaging and Event Streaming

Monitoring: As Microservices are distributed and heterogeneous in nature, it is critical to monitor and visualize making sure that software is reliable, available, and performs as expected. Monitoring typically involves collecting metrics from all the applicable systems involved and analyzing/visualizing call graphs. These gets complex as the application complexity (again depends on number Microservices and their interactions in a call graph) grows. There are many commercial and open source tools for monitoring Microservices.

Distributed Tracing: Distributed tracing helps in how a request travels through the application, especially when team may not have any insight into the implementation of the calling Microservice. Tracing tools introduces unique IDs to logging which are consistent between Microservice calls which makes it possible to find how a single request travels from one Microservice to the next. This is how the visualization of the parent / child relationship of span would look like

Security: Access to Microservices needs to be protected. Distributed nature of Microservices pose more challenges in terms of securing the endpoints. Security Frameworks like oAuth2 address the security concern. There are multiple ways of configuring security for Microservices; by making API Gateway behave like reverse proxy or by securing each Microservice using the security service (backing service like IAM) provided by the PaaS provider.

Backing Services: A PaaS provider will provide services grouped into various categories like database, analytics, security, Data warehouse etc. to be used by the cloud application. These services will be exposed on lightweight protocols (like REST) and can be consumed by the cloud application by binding. PaaS providers provide consoles (UI based) to manage backing services.

On Premise Integration: Typically, API Gateway will be used to mediate the communication between cloud and on premise applications. API Services will be used to orchestrate calls that span cloud and on premise by calling the enterprise integration infrastructure for calling any applications on premise.

Infrastructure: Infrastructure has two components; PaaS and IaaS. IaaS is the abstraction onto the hardware and provides on demand resource provisioning. Resources can be scaled out or in based on the usage pattern. PaaS is cloud platform residing on top of IaaS. This layer provides the required support for the cloud applications to deploy and run. PaaS provides various runtimes and many backing services required for a cloud application.

3.7 Microservices based LMS Architecture

LMS has standardized on an MSA Reference Architecture and a framework that each of the Microservices teams will leverage.

The various modules / sub modules in Business Logic Layers are developed as Microservices as shown in the diagram below. Also, the API shall operate on specific domain objects and not depend on request/response objects of Presentation Layer. For example, Prepare API shall accept the inputs in the form of prepare domain object, user Information API say can have createapplicant API, updateapplicant API, viewapplicant API which shall accept the inputs in the form of License domain object. It should be possible to easily expose this re-usable APIs as services when required.

User registration, License Management, Reports & analytics are to be developed as reusable components which can be leveraged by various departments.

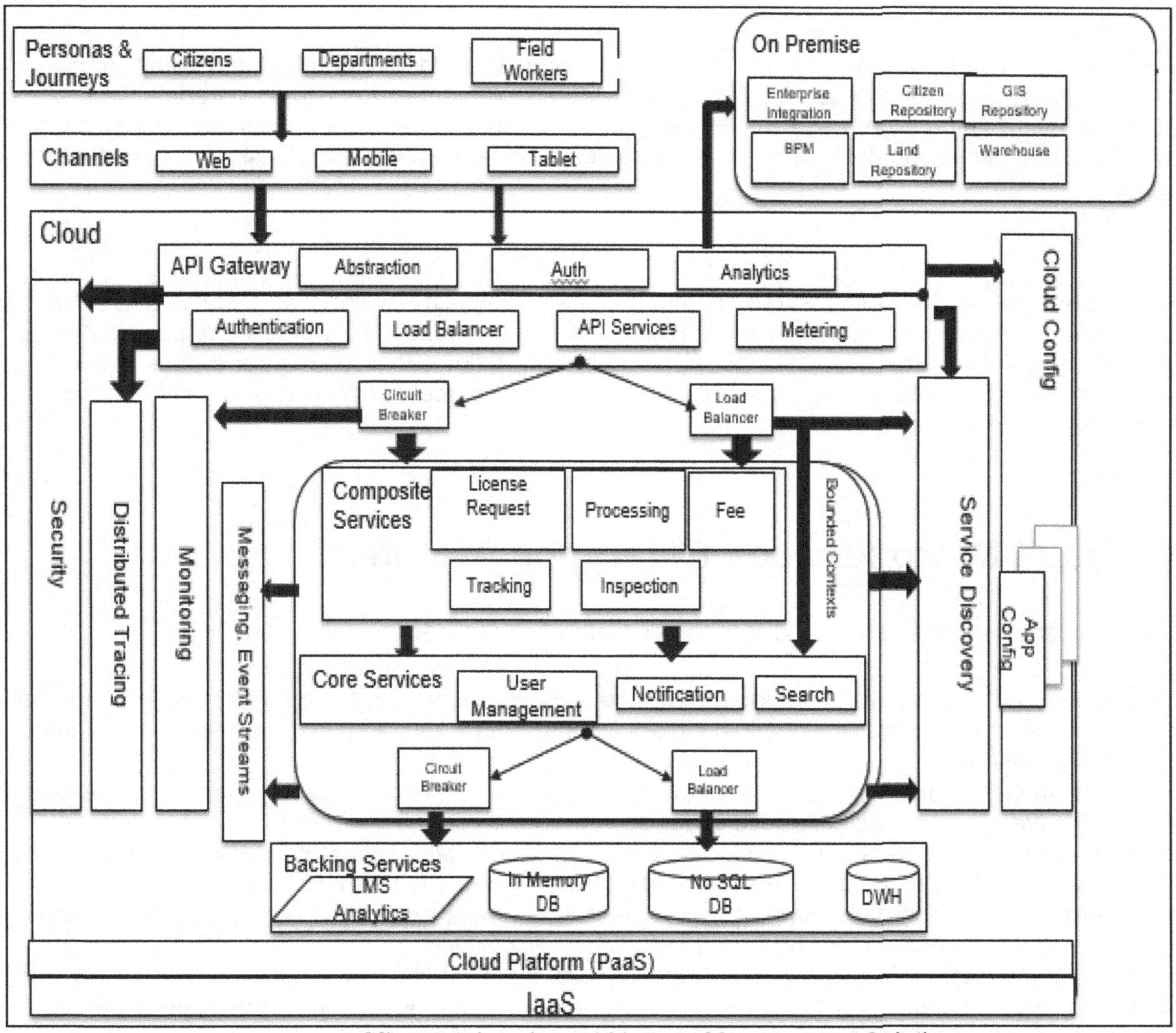

Microservices based License Management Solution

User Registration Microservice

This Microservice allows the user to log in. It validates the user's identification and security credentials, and ensures the account is valid based on a set of business rules. The Microservice API accepts an encrypted data object consisting of user credentials and account information. It queries the enterprise Identity and Access Management (IAM) solutions to validate the user credentials. It retrieves the user authentication token and account identifier.

License Request Microservice

This Microservice request for the fresh, renewal, amendment and transfer of license/ permits as desired by the applicant. It provides a customized list of licenses, permits, and regulations that are required or need to comply with across all levels of government. It supports an interface that allows applicants to upload License/ permit application documents at administrator – specified points in the workflow.

Fee Processing Microservice

This Microservice support Setting up of the Fees, Payments and Refunds for Permits and Licenses. It is able to support all fees, fee tables, and fee information based on permit type, including effective and expire dates, shared fee variables, and unique fee variables where needed.

License processing

This Microservice is able to replicate or transfer common information to other applications. Examples include Renewal - Money Lending License is directed to Police Department, Revenue, Registration, People Repository departments/applications. It automatically assigns inspections based on location or other business rules. Also, it automatically assigns due/completion dates to reviews, inspections, and other events and tasks in License/ permit and workflows.

Inspection

This Microservice able to request inspections through different mediums such as telephone, On-line and software by responsible party and inspectors. It automatically triggers an inspection based on scheduling or performance of another inspection type on the same or related permit. It creates workflows to document and track associated preliminary applications such as exemption requests and similar early processes that may or may not become part of a subsequent License/Permit application.

3.8 Benefits of Microservices Reference Architecture

The following are the benefits of the usage of Microservices Reference Architecture,

- **Independent deployments**: we can update a service without redeploying the entire application, and roll back or roll forward an update if something goes wrong. Bug fixes and feature releases are more manageable and less risk
- **Independent development**: A single development team can build, test, and deploy a service. The result is continuous innovation and a faster release cadence
- **Small, focused teams**: Teams can focus on one service. The smaller scope of each service makes the code base easier to understand, and it's easier for new team members to ramp up
- **Fault isolation:** If a service goes down, it won't take out the entire application. We can follow resiliency best practices and design patterns for fault isolation
- **Mixed technology stacks**. Teams can pick the technology that best fits their service
- **Granular scaling**. Services can be scaled independently. At the same time, the higher density of services per VM means that VM resources are fully utilized. Using placement constraints, a services can be matched to a VM profile (high CPU, high memory, and so on)

3.9 Best Practices of Microservices Reference Architecture

The following are the high level Microservices Reference Architecture best practices,

- Model services around the business domain.
- Decentralize everything. Individual teams are responsible for designing and building services. Avoid sharing code or data schemas.
- Data storage should be private to the service that owns the data. Use the best storage for each service and data type.
- Services communicate through well-designed APIs. Avoid leaking implementation details. APIs should model the domain, not the internal implementation of the service.
- Avoid coupling between services. Causes of coupling include shared database schemas and rigid communication protocols.
- Offload cross-cutting concerns, such as authentication and SSL termination, to the gateway.
- Keep domain knowledge out of the gateway. The gateway should handle and route client requests without any knowledge of the business rules or domain logic. Otherwise, the gateway becomes a dependency and can cause coupling between services.
- Services should have loose coupling and high functional cohesion. Functions that are likely to change together should be packaged and deployed together. If they reside in separate services, those services

end up being tightly coupled, because a change in one service will require updating the other service. Overly chatty communication between two services may be a symptom of tight coupling and low cohesion.

- Isolate failures. Use resiliency strategies to prevent failures within a service from cascading.

3.10 Summary

Microservices is not a product, framework, or platform. It is a strategy for building large enterprise distributed systems. One of the characteristic of Microservice is of loosely coupled and deployed independently of one another. Microservices architecture can offer enterprises many advantages, from independent scalability of diverse application components to faster, easier software development and maintenance. Sizing of the Microservices is very critical for the design of the better services. Open source technology solutions and organizational methods are leading the Microservices market. As a result, Microservices reduce vendor lock-in and eliminate long-term technology commitment, helps to choose the tools need to meet IT and business goals.

Microservices Reference Architecture depicted in this chapter,

- Provides ready-to-use blueprints for building Microservices based systems, speeding – and improving – development
- Create a platform for testing new features, whether developed internally or externally
- Helps understand partner systems and components to enterprises to gain a holistic perspective on the Microservices ecosystem

In addition, Microservices Reference Architecture need to be developed based on industry-standard components like Docker containers, and a wide range of languages – Java, PHP, Python, Node.js/JavaScript and Ruby etc. Developed Microservice must expose JavaScript Object Notation (JSON) or Extensible Mark up Language (XML) over the HTTP to provide a REST API. These standards would provide guidelines about how to describe, maintain, and retire Microservices.

Finally, Microservices based System Design is an ongoing story. It is not something that has to done once, and immediately. With the right people, processes, and tools, Microservices can deliver faster development and deployment, easier maintenance, improved scalability, and freedom from long-term technology commitment.

4. Microservices Patterns

There are many patterns related to the Microservices Architecture. Following are some popular patterns used by applications built using Microservices architecture.

The following diagram shows the holistic view of the Microservices Pattern commonly used across the enterprise.

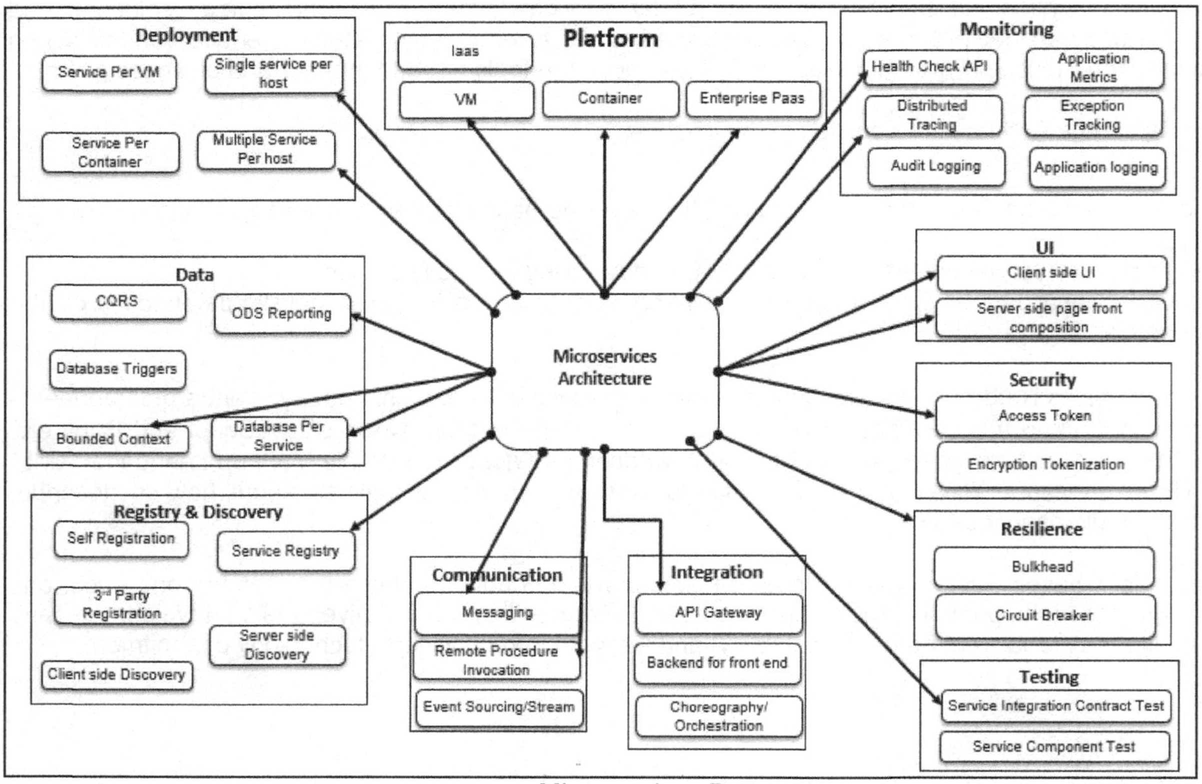

Microservices Patterns

The various categories of Patterns are explained below.

4.1 Deployment

Microservices application consists of many services. Services are written in a variety of languages and frameworks. Each one with its own specific deployment, resource, scaling, and monitoring requirements. There will be need to run a certain number of instances of each service based on the demand for that service. Also, each service instance must be provisioned with the appropriate CPU, memory, and I/O resources. Challenging aspect is that despite this complexity, deploying services must be fast, reliable and cost-effective. There are a few different Microservice deployment patterns explained below.

Service Per VM

This pattern talks about deploying the service as one service instance per VM. The drivers for this pattern are,

* Service must be independently deployable and scalable
* Service instances isolation
* Quickly build and deploy a service
* Constrain the resources (CPU and memory) consumed by a service
* Monitor the behavior of each service instance

The following diagram shows the structure of this pattern:

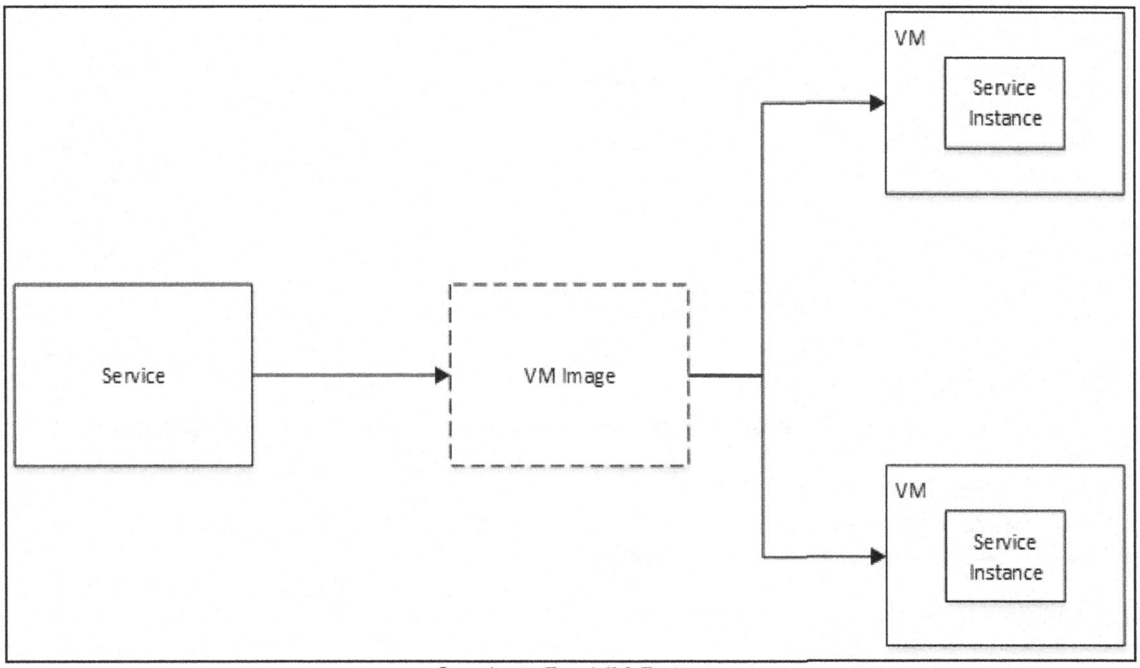

Services Per VM Pattern

Single service Instance per Host

This pattern talks about deploying the service as one service instance per host. Below are the drivers:

* Service instances isolation
* No possibility of conflicting resource requirements or dependency versions
* To constraint the resources of a single host
* Easier to monitor, manage, and redeploy each service instance

The following diagram shows the structure of this pattern,

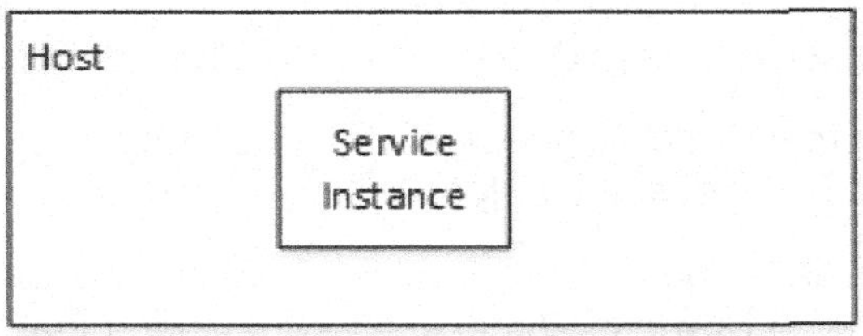

Single Instance Pattern

Service Instance Per Container

This pattern talks about deploying the service as one service instance per container. Below are the drivers,

* Containers are quick to build and start
* Easier to scale up and down a service by changing the number of container instances.
* Service instance is isolation

The following diagram shows the structure of this pattern:

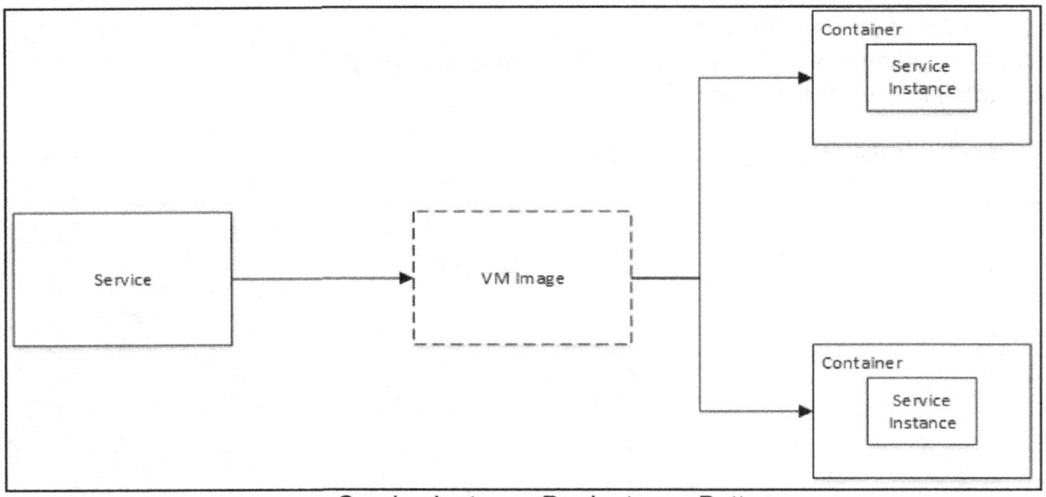

Service Instance Per Instance Pattern

Multiple Service Instance Per host

This pattern talks about deploying different services (instances) per host. Below points describe the drivers,

- Efficient resource utilization
- Service instance isolation
- Monitor the behavior of each service instance

The following diagram shows the structure of this pattern.

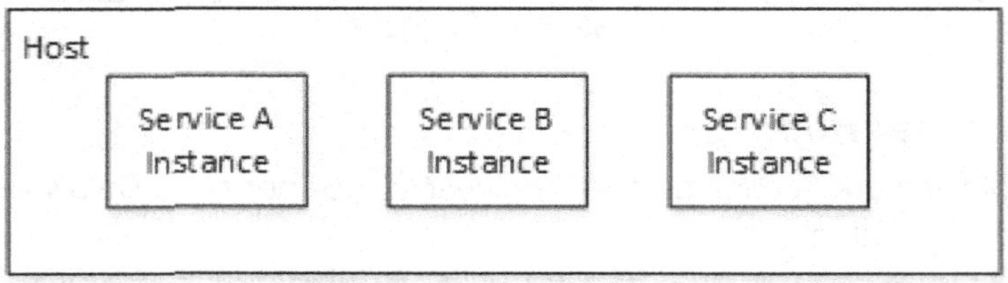

Multiple Service Instance Pattern

Serverless Deployment

A deployment infrastructure that hides the concept of - physical or virtual hosts, or containers. The infrastructure takes service code and runs it. Consumer charged for each request based on the resources consumed.

To deploy service using this approach, code needs to be packaged (e.g. as a ZIP file), uploaded to the deployment infrastructure and specify the desired performance characteristics.

The deployment infrastructure is usually operated by a public cloud provider. It typically uses either containers or virtual machines to isolate the services. However, these details are hidden from the users.

4.2 Platform

Use a deployment platform, which is automated infrastructure for application deployment. It provides a service abstraction, which is a set of highly available (e.g. load balanced) service instances. Examples are: Docker Swarm, Kubernetes etc.

Below are options available for Microservices to use as a deployment platform. Each application can choose one of the option based on the applicability or requirement

Iaas

Cloud infrastructure services, known as Infrastructure as a Service (IaaS), are self-service models for accessing, monitoring, and managing remote datacenter infrastructures, such as compute (virtualized or bare metal), storage, networking, and networking services (e.g. firewalls). Instead of having to purchase hardware outright, users can purchase IaaS based on consumption.

VM

A virtual machine is a software computer that, like a physical computer, runs an operating system and applications. The virtual machine is comprised of a set of specification and configuration files and is backed by the physical resources of a host. Every virtual machine has virtual devices that provide the same functionality as physical hardware and have additional benefits in terms of portability, manageability, and security.

Container

A container is a lightweight, stand-alone, executable package of a piece of software that includes everything needed to run it: code, runtime, system tools, system libraries, settings. Available for both Linux and Windows based apps, containerized software will always run the same, regardless of the environment. Containers isolate software from its surroundings

Enterprise PaaS

Enterprise PaaS refers to the internal application of the platform as a service model, with the goal of boosting software productivity through standardized developer tools and common components. This is PaaS applied internally in an enterprise, a private PaaS.

4.3 Monitoring

As Microservices are distributed and heterogeneous in nature, it is critical to monitor and visualize making sure that software is reliable, available, and performs as expected. Monitoring typically involves collecting metrics from all the applicable systems involved and analyzing/visualizing call graphs. Below are various means to monitor.

Health check API

This pattern determines health of a service. A service has health check API endpoint (e.g. HTTP /health) that returns the health of the service. The API endpoint handler performs various checks, such as,

- the status of the connections to the infrastructure services used by the service instance
- the status of the host, e.g. disk space
- application specific requirements

Application Metrics

Application-level metrics help developers investigate and diagnose issues with their applications running on cloud platforms. Instrument a service to gather statistics about individual operations. Aggregate metrics in centralized metrics service, which provides reporting and alerting. There are two models for aggregating metrics:

- push - the service pushes metrics to the metrics service
- pull - the metrics services pull metrics from the service

Below are few important application metrics:

- Response Time
- Throughput
- Request Duration

- Memory Usage
- Events (Threshold alerting)

Distributed Tracing

One of the problems developer's encounter as their Microservice applications grow is tracing requests that propagate from one Microservice to the next. It will be difficult to figure out how a request travels through the application, especially when there is no insight into the implementation of the Microservice. Tracing tools introduces unique IDs to logging which are consistent between Microservice calls which makes it possible to find how a single request travels from one Microservice to the next.

Distributed tracing tools barrows Dapper's terminology - A Dapper trace represents a tree of activity across multiple services.

Span - The basic unit of work

a) Spans are started and stopped
b) They keep track of their timing information
c) Once a span is created, it must be stopped at some point of time in the future
d) Has a parent and can have multiple children

Trace – A set of spans forming a tree-like structure. Nodes in the trace tree are spans

Log events / Annotations – Annotations is used to record existence of an event in time. Some of the core annotations used to define the start and stop of a request are:

a) Client Sent - The client has made a request. This annotation depicts the start of the span.
b) Server Received – This indicates that server received the request and will start processing. Network latency is the difference between 'Client Sent' timestamp and "Server Received" timestamp.
c) Server Sent - Annotated upon completion of request processing (when the response sent back to the client). Time needed by the server side to process the request is the difference between 'Server Received' timestamp and "Server Sent" timestamp.
d) Client Received - Signifies the end of the span. The client has successfully received the response from the server side. Whole time needed by the client to receive the response from the server is the difference between 'Client Sent' timestamp and "Client Received" timestamp.

Below figure depicts Trace and Span will look in a system together with annotations.

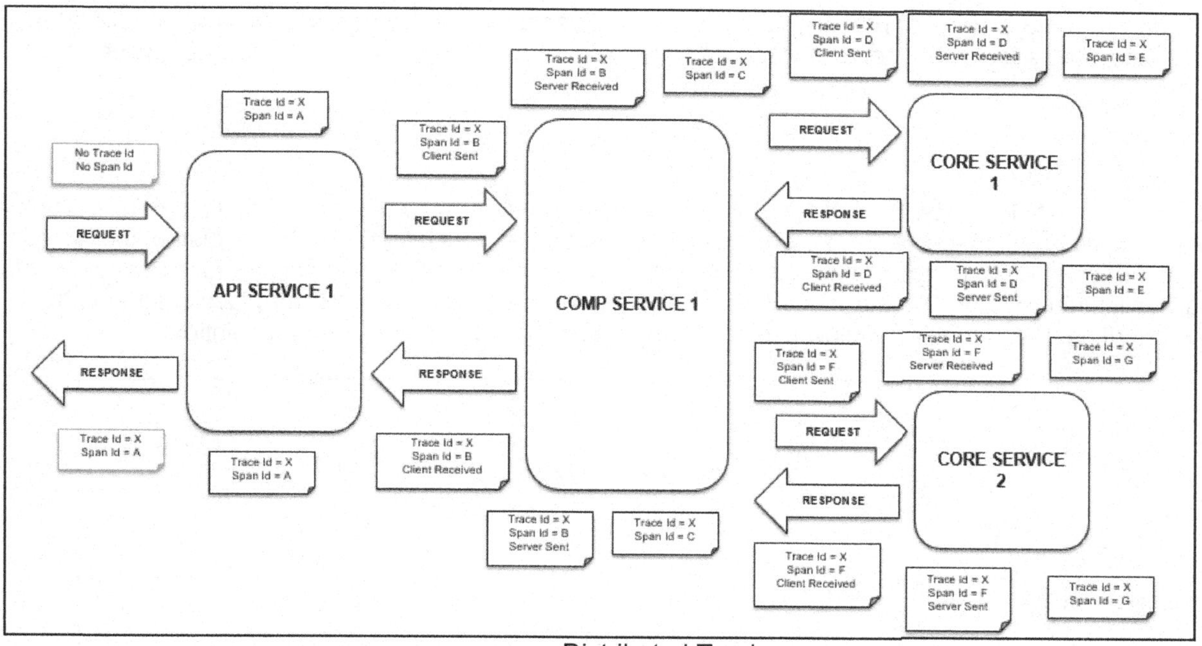

Distributed Tracing

This is how the visualization of the parent / child relationship of span would look like

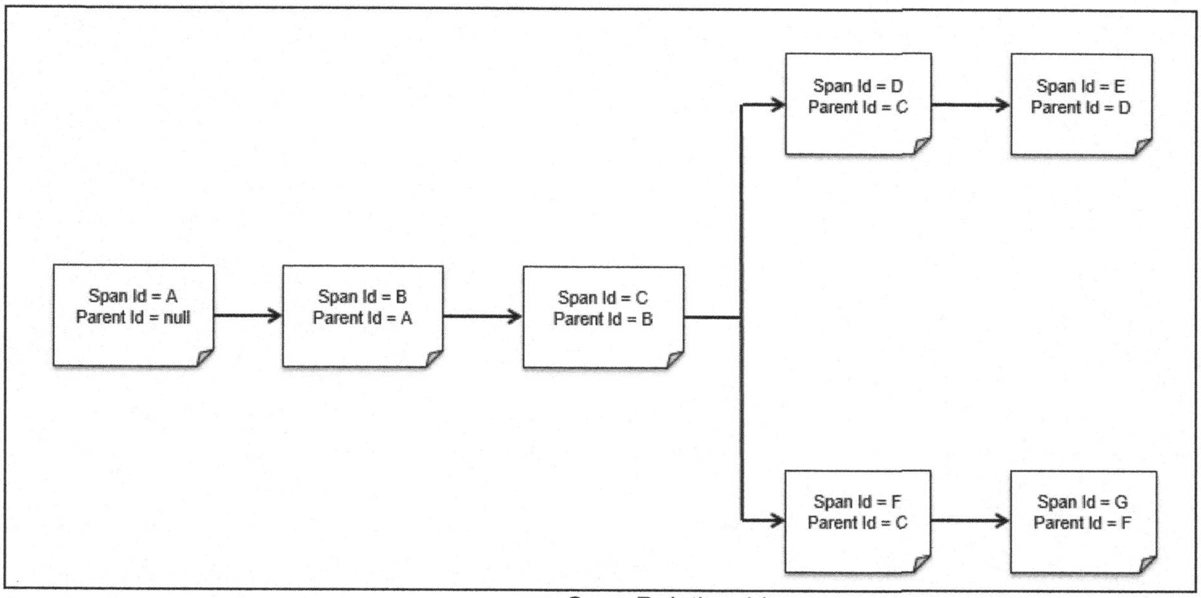

Span Relationship

Exception Tracking

Microservices are distributed in nature, tracking an exception becomes very difficult. As the request, flow travels through the application, especially when there is no insight into the implementation of the Microservice, any exceptions/errors from the invocations must be de-duplicated, recorded at a centralized exception tracking service that aggregates and tracks exceptions and notifies developers.

Audit Logging

An audit log is the simplest, yet also one of the most effective forms of tracking activity information. The idea is that any time significant activity happens the activity is recorded indicating what happened, when it happened and who did it. Generally, audit information is written to a physical file. Writing the audit log to a centralized data store into a simple audit trail table is another practice. Log management solution involves getting the logs generated by various microservices into a log appender and there to the logging infrastructure like ELK for further analysis.

Application Logging

Microservices run on multiple hosts. To fulfill a single business requirement, we might need to talk to multiple services running on different machines. The log messages generated by Microservices are distributed across multiple hosts. Correlating among logs generated by different Microservices will be a challenge for developers. All the generated application logs across the hosts should be sent to an external, centralized place. Log structured data and use correlation IDs for tracing. Below is the diagram depicting the log management solution.

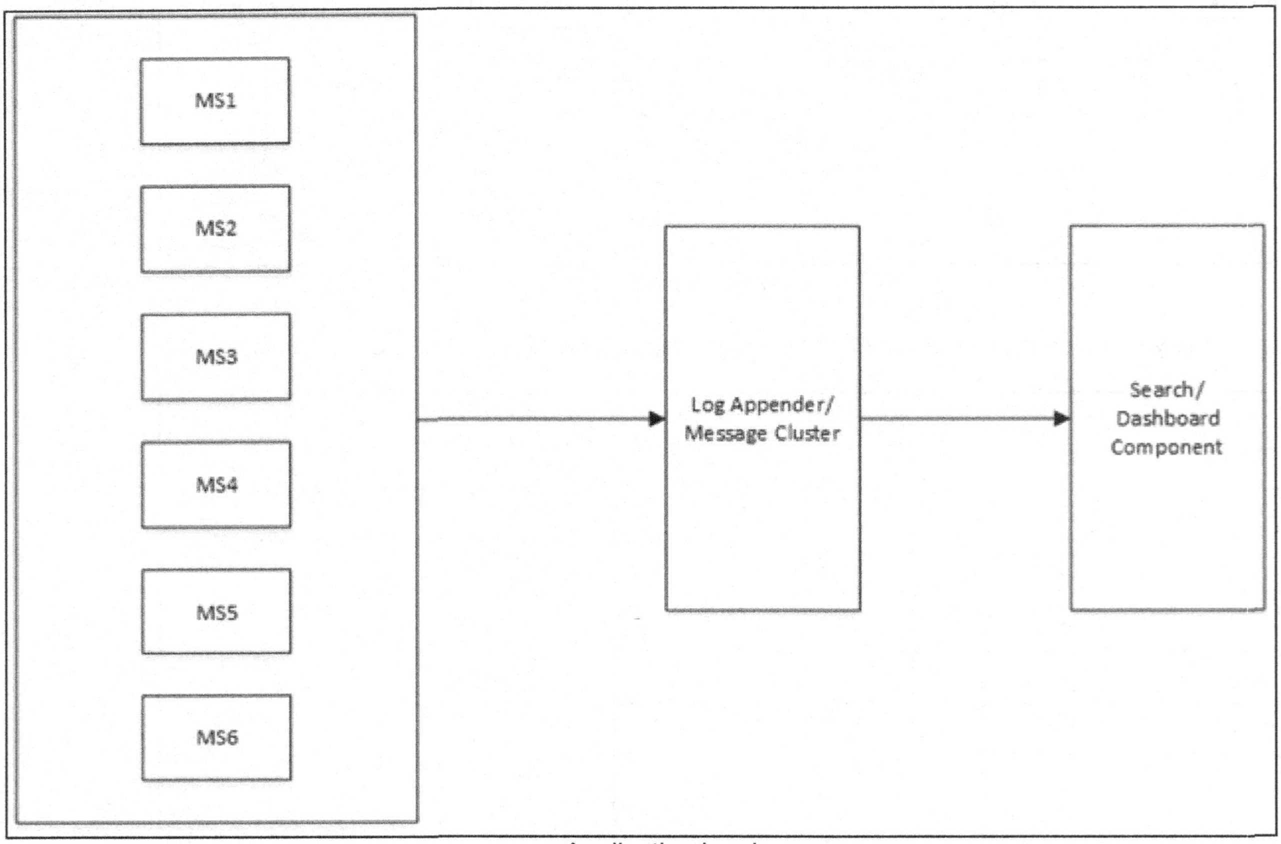

Application logging

Examples for above solution are: Kafka Log Appender/Cluster, ELK for search and dashboard.

4.4 Data

This section describes various data architecture patterns used in Microservices for specific purposes.

CQRS

CQRS stands for Command Query Responsibility Segregation. At its heart is the notion that different model can be used to update information than the model used to read information. The change that CQRS introduces is to split that conceptual model into separate models (object models) for update and display, which it refers to as Command and Query respectively. CQRS fits well with event-based programming models. This pattern was first introduced by Greg Young and Udi Dahan. They took inspiration from a pattern called Command Query Separation which was defined by Bertrand Meyer in his book "Object Oriented Software Construction". The main idea behind CQS is: "A method should either change state of an object, or return a result, but not both. In other words, asking the question should not change the answer. More formally, methods should return a value only if they are referentially transparent and hence possess no side effects." A method is divided into two sets:

- Commands - change the state of an object or entire system (sometimes called as modifiers or mutators).
- Queries - return results and do not change the state of an object.

Below diagram represents Command Query Responsibility Segregation:

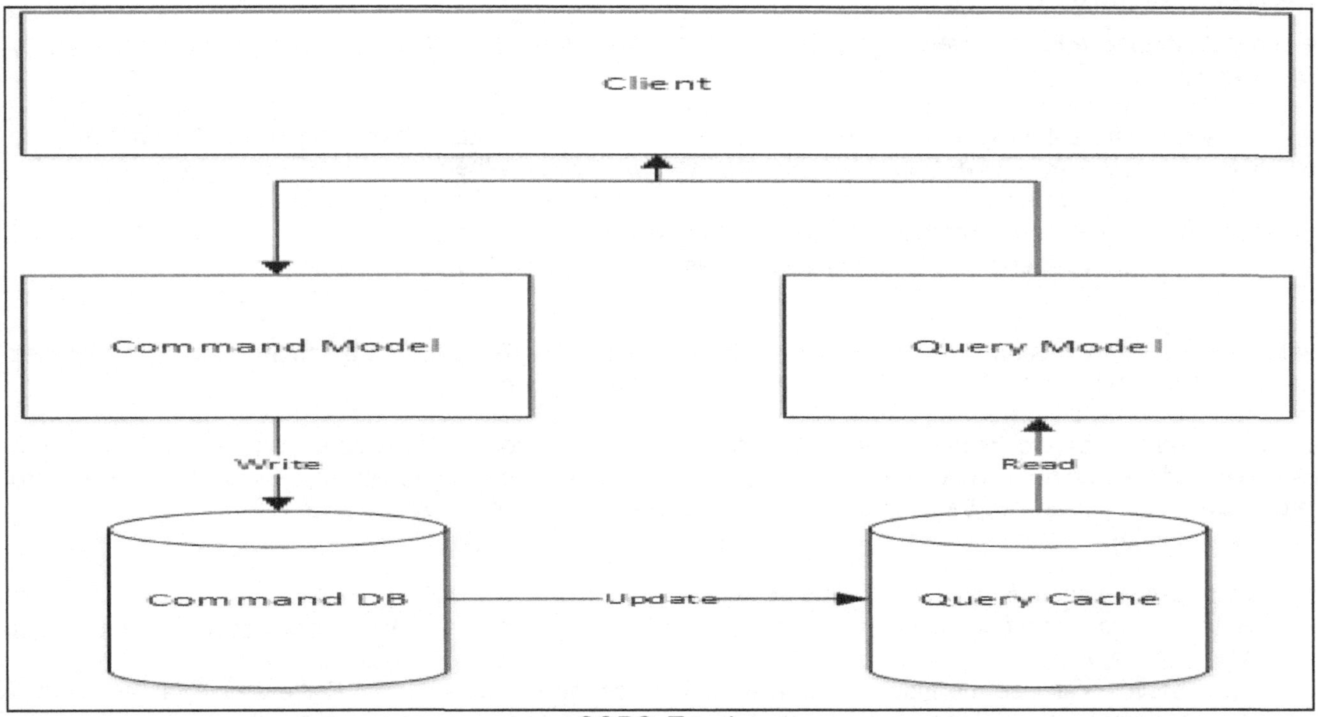

CQRS Topology

The query model used to fetch the data and command model to modify. This pattern is broadly applicable and it makes reasoning about objects easier. On the other hand, CQRS is applicable only on specific problems.

Many applications that use mainstream approaches consists of models, which are common for read and write side. Having the same model for read and write side leads to a more complex model that could be very difficult to maintain and optimize.

The real strength of these two patterns is that methods can be separated that change state from those that don't. This separation could be very handy in situations of performance and tuning. Read side of the system can be optimized independently from the write side. The write side is known as the domain. The domain contains all the behavior. The read side is specialized for reporting needs.

Another benefit of this pattern is in the case of large applications. Developers can be divided into smaller teams working on different sides of the system (read or write) without knowledge of the other side. For example developers working on read side do not need to understand the domain model.

Database Triggers

In order to be reliable, services must atomically publish events whenever their state changes. It is not viable to use a distributed transaction that spans the database and the message broker. One or more database triggers insert events into an EVENTS table, which is polled by a separate process that publishes the events.

Bounded Context

Any sophisticated business domain consists of one or more bounded contexts, each responsible for one part of the domain. A bounded context contains models describing the domain and is a boundary for the meaning of these models. A model should be small enough to be assigned to one team. A bounded context clarifies, encapsulates, and defines the specific responsibility to the model. It ensures the domain is not distracted from the outside. Each model must have a context implicitly defined within a sub-domain, and every context defines boundaries.

Database per Service

The service's database is effectively part of the implementation of that service. It cannot be accessed directly by other services.

There are a few different ways to keep a service's persistent data private. A database server for each service need not to be provisioned. For example, if a relational database is used then the options are:

- Private-tables-per-service – Each service owns a set of tables that's only be accessed by that service
- Schema-per-service – Each service has a database schema that's private
- Database-server-per-service – Each service has own database server.

Private-tables-per-service and schema-per-service have very low overhead. Using a schema per service makes ownership clearer. Some services might need their own database server.

It is a good idea to create constraints that enforce this modularity. Different database user id can be assigned to each service and use database access control mechanism such as grants. Without some kind of constraints to enforce, developers will always be tempted to bypass a service's API and access its data directly.

Using a database per service has the following benefits:

- Helps ensure that the services are loosely coupled. Changes to one service's database does not impact any other services.
- Each service can use the type of database that is best suited to its needs. For example, a service that does text searches could use ElasticSearch. A service that manipulates a social graph could use Neo4j.

4.5 Communication

This section describes various communication patterns like messaging and remote procedure call used in Microservices for specific purposes.

Messaging

With asynchronous messaging for inter service communication, the service consumer makes a request, but does not wait for the operation to complete. As soon as the request is acknowledged, the service consumer moves on. This type of interaction allows publish/subscribe style of service communication.
Asynchronous communication can be very useful for long-running jobs, where keeping a connection open for a long period between the client and server is impractical. It also works very well when low latency is required, where blocking a call while waiting for the result can slow things down. Due to the nature of mobile networks and devices, firing off requests and assuming things have worked (unless told otherwise) can ensure that the UI remains responsive even if the network has high latency.

This pattern has the following benefits:

- Loose coupling: It decouples consumer from services
- Improved availability since the message broker buffers messages until the consumer is able to consume them

- Supports a variety of communication patterns including request/reply, notifications, request/async response, publish/subscribe, publish/async response etc.

Remote Procedure Call

Services must handle requests from the application's clients. Furthermore, services must sometimes collaborate to handle those requests, remote procedure invocation is used for inter process (service) communication. The client uses a request/reply-based protocol to make requests to a service. Following are the benefits:

- Simple and familiar
- Request/reply is easy
- Simpler system since there in no intermediate broker

4.6 Integration

This section highlights various integration patterns like API Gateway, choreography and orchestration.

API Gateway / Backend for Front end

In Microservice architecture, multiple clients could make requests to each of the Microservices directly. The clients communicate with individual services and thereby have to communicate with many different services to aggregate the data internally upon reception of responses from these services.

Unfortunately, there are challenges and limitations with this option. One problem is the mismatch between the needs of the client and the fine-grained APIs exposed by each of the Microservices. Another problem with the client directly calling the Microservices is that some might use protocols that are not web-friendly. One service might use Thrift binary RPC while another service might use the AMQP messaging protocol. Neither of the protocol is particularly browser or firewall friendly and is best used internally. An application should use protocols such as HTTP and WebSocket outside of the firewall. Another drawback with this approach is that it makes difficult to refactor the Microservices. Over time, there might be a need to change how the system is partitioned into services.

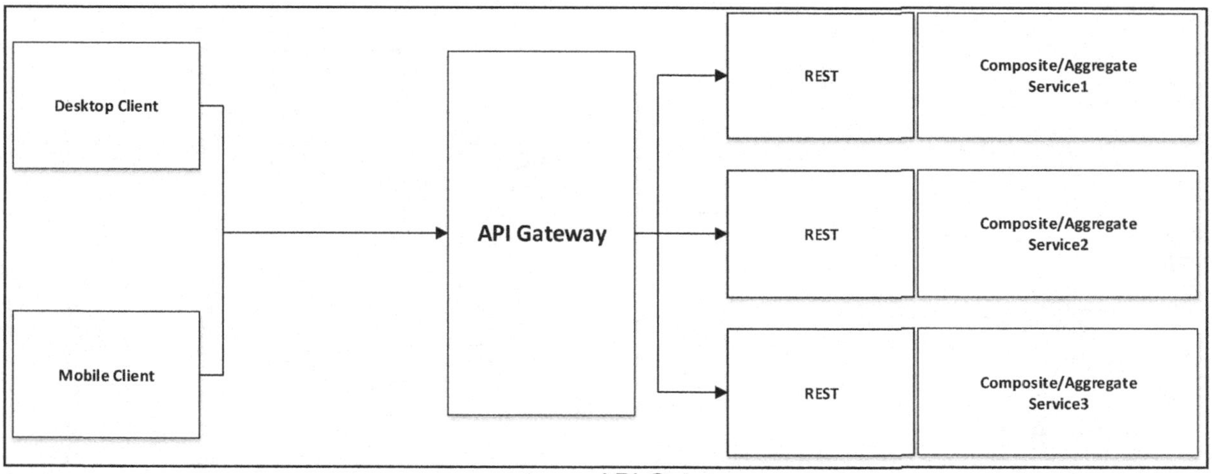

API Gateway

API gateway is the single entry point for all clients. API Gateway is responsible for aggregating data or, in some cases, acting as a simple routing layer for appropriate services. The API gateway can be seen as a single point of failure. A better approach may be to create multiple API gateways for the different platform or frontends that the application needs to support.

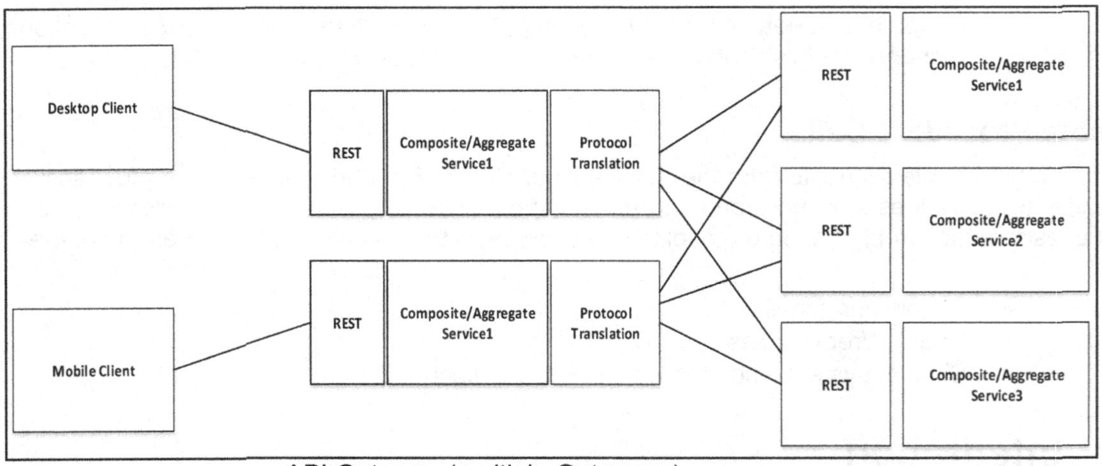

API Gateway (multiple Gateways)

4.7 Registry & Discovery

Service Discovery

Microservices typically depend on each other to complete a task. In order to make a request, the code needs to know the location i.e. IP address and port of a service instance.

For example, consider, the composite service 1-client calls composite service 1 then, the code can read the network locations from a configuration file.

If location of one of the instance of composite service 1 changes then update configuration file so that comp service 1 client can find the new service instance. This solution is not scalable solution and very difficult in maintaining the application that consists of many Microservices.

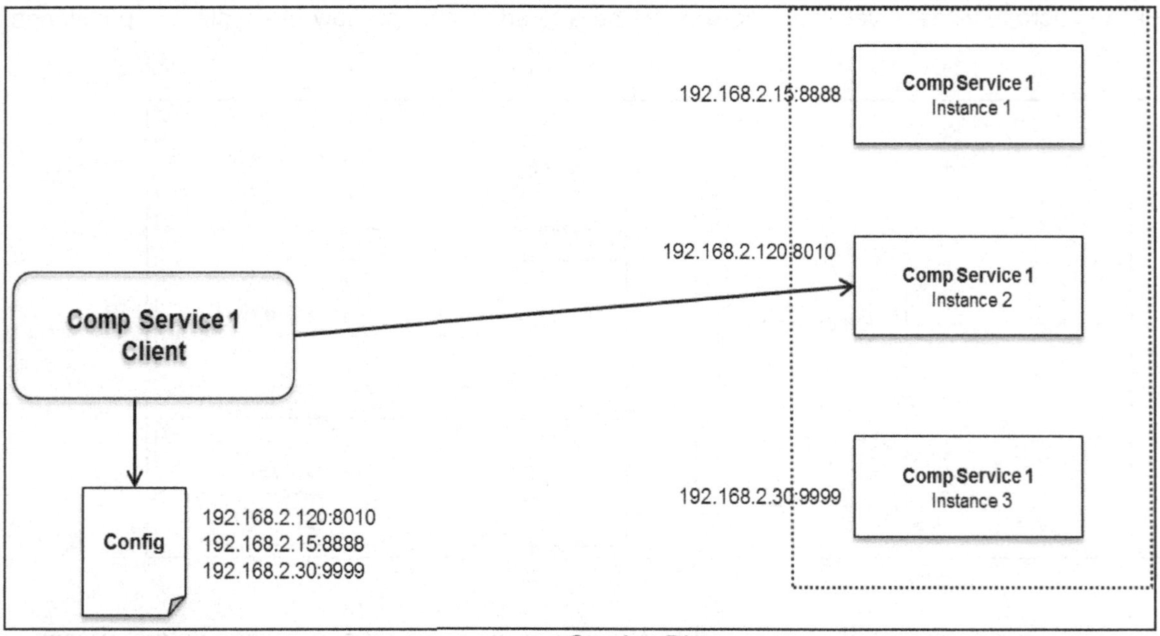

Service Discovery

In cloud-based Microservices application, service instances have dynamically assigned network locations. Moreover, service instances change dynamically because of auto-scaling, failures, and upgrades. The client code needs to use a service discovery mechanism.

There are two main service discovery patterns: Client-side discovery and Server-side discovery.

Client-Side Discovery Pattern

The client is responsible for determining the network locations of available service instances and load balancing requests across them. The client queries a service registry, which is a database of available service instances. The client then uses a load-balancing algorithm to select one of the available service instances and makes a request.

The following diagram shows the structure of this pattern.

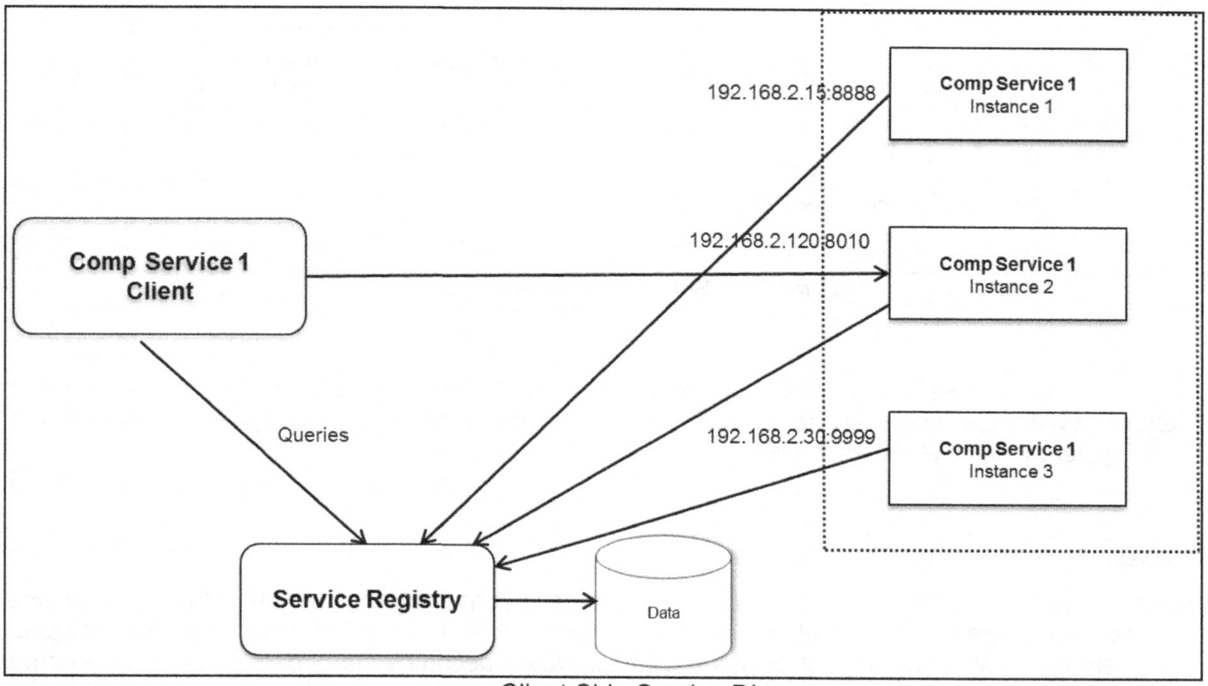

Client Side Service Discovery

The network location of a service instance is registered with the service registry when it starts up. It is removed from the service registry when the instance terminates. The service instance's registration is refreshed periodically using a heartbeat mechanism.

Server-Side Discovery Pattern

The other approach to service discovery is the server-side discovery pattern. The following diagram shows the structure of this pattern.

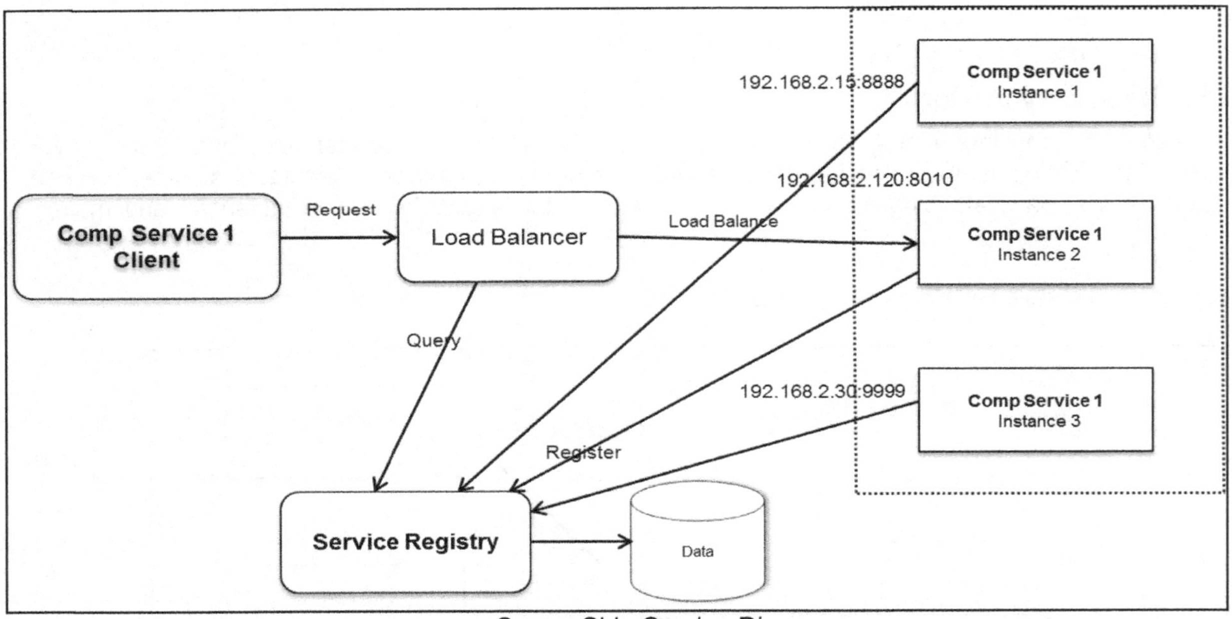

Server Side Service Discovery

The client makes a request to a service via a load balancer. The load balancer queries the service registry and routes each request to an available service instance. As with client-side discovery, service instances are registered and deregistered with the service registry.

Service Registry

The service registry is a key part of service discovery. It is a database containing the network locations of service instances. A service registry needs to be highly available and up to date. Clients can cache network locations obtained from the service registry. However, that information eventually becomes out of date and clients become unable to discover service instances. Consequently, a service registry consists of a cluster of servers that use a replication protocol to maintain consistency.

Service Registration Options

Service instances must be registered with and deregistered from the service registry. There are a couple of different ways to handle the registration and deregistration. One option is for service instances to register themselves, the self-registration pattern. The other option is for third party system component to manage the registration of service instances, the third-party registration pattern.

Self-Registration Pattern

Self-registration forces Microservices to interact with the service registry by themselves. In this pattern service instance is responsible for registering and deregistering itself with the service registry. Also, if required, a service instance sends heartbeat requests to prevent its registration from expiring. The following diagram shows the structure of this pattern.

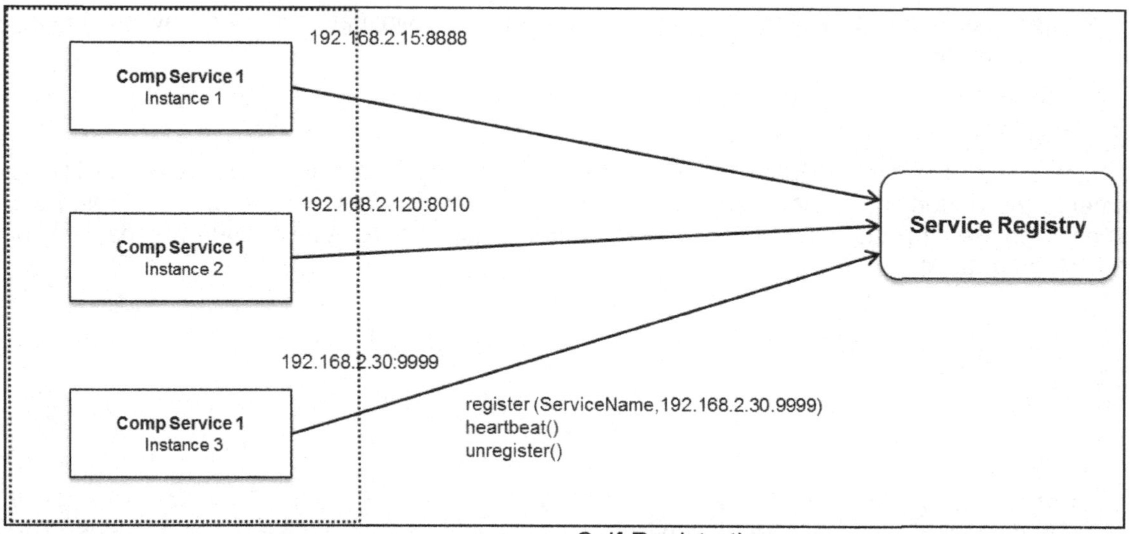

Self-Registration

Third-Party Registration Pattern

In this case, a third party process or service manages all other services. Service instances are not responsible for registering themselves with the service registry. Instead, another system component known as the service registrar handles the registration. The service registrar tracks changes to the set of running instances by either polling the deployment environment or subscribing to events. When it notices a newly available service instance, it registers the instance with the service registry. The service registrar also deregisters terminated service instances.

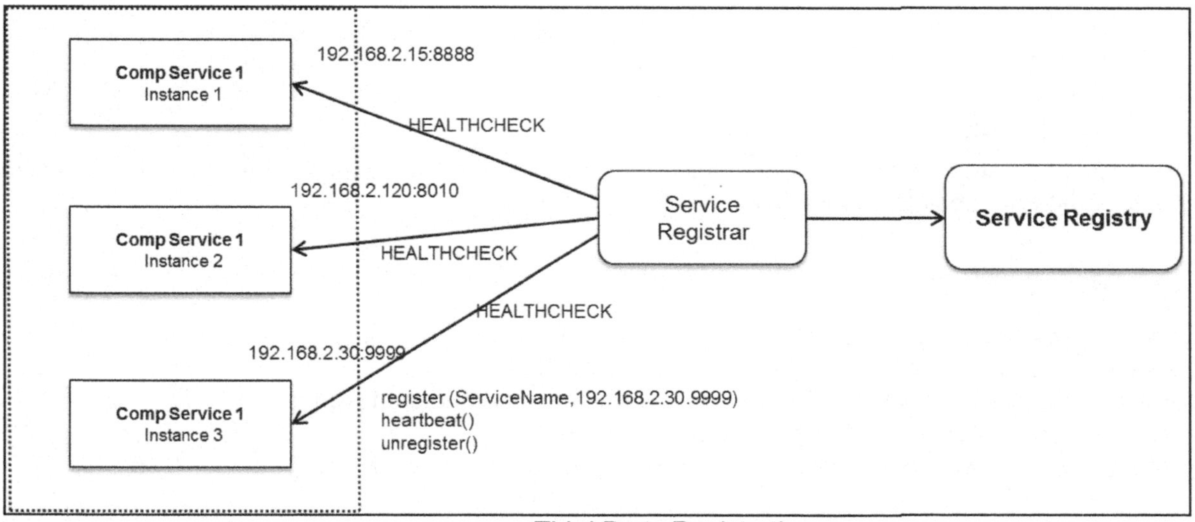

Third Party Registration

4.8 UI

This section highlights UI patterns for frontend developers to aggregate the data from multiple services and display on a page at client side or doing the same at the server side.

Client side UI Composition

Services are developed by business capability/subdomain-oriented teams that are also responsible for the user experience. Some UI screens/pages display data from multiple service. Client side UI composition pattern addresses the problem of how to display a page that gets data from multiple services. Each team develops a client-side UI component, such an AngularJS directive that implements the region of the page/screen for their service. A UI team is responsible implementing the page skeletons that build pages/screens by composing multiple, service-specific UI components.

Server side page fragment composition

This pattern is an alternative to the above. Each team develops a web application that generates the HTML fragment that implements the region of the page for their service. A UI team is responsible for developing the page templates that build pages by performing server-side aggregation (like server-side include mechanism) of the service-specific HTML fragments.

4.9 Security

Access Token

An application consists of numerous services. The API gateway is the single entry point for client requests. It authenticates requests, and forwards them to other services, which might in turn invoke other services. The problem is how and who will communicate the identity of the requestor of the service? API Gateway authenticates the request and passes an access token (e.g. JSON Web Token) that securely identifies the requestor in each request to the services. A service can include the access token in requests it makes to other services.

This pattern has the following benefits:

- The identity of the requestor is securely passed around the system
- Services can verify that the requestor is authorized to perform an operation

Encryption / Tokenization

Tokenization and encryption are two ways for securing information – while transmission and while at rest. They are not the same thing and are not interchangeable.

Tokenization

- Uses 'tokens' to protect data.
- Tokens serve as references or placeholders for the original data.
- Uses a database, called a 'token vault', which stores the real data and the token.
- Token interception cannot be used to guess the real values.
- Primary benefit is ease of use, encryption keys do not have to be managed.

Encryption

- Uses 'secret keys' to protect data.
- Uses an algorithm to transform plain text information into a non-readable form called cipher text.
- Needs an encryption key to decrypt the information and return it to its original plain text form.
- If private key is intercepted, it can be used to decrypt all of the data.

4.10 Resiliency

Below section provides couple of resiliency patterns to make the application resilient and avoid failure of entire application because of failure in one part of the system. It also talks about monitoring a service to make sure that it does not degrade beyond a specified threshold.

Bulkhead

In general, the goal of the bulkhead pattern is to avoid faults in one part of a system to take the entire system down. The term comes from ships where a ship is divided in separate watertight compartments to avoid a single hull breach to flood the entire ship; it will only flood one bulkhead.

When designing application with Microservices, we should place bulkheads in appropriate locations so that an error in one location does not escalate to other parts of the ecosystem.

Below are few principles with examples:

- **Design for redundancy**. Redundancy is critical here, example a farm of servers behind load-balancers. One server failure does not affect others.
- **Application partitioning** based on criticality. Make sure that critical applications are properly isolated.
- **Design with isolation.** If every Microservice in the ecosystem depends on one DB, a failure in DB will bring down the whole ecosystem. As much as possible, need to make the Microservices autonomous.
- **Fail fast.** Take for example a method X of service A depending on method Y in another service B. Assume service B fails. Method X in service A does not have timeout/fallback defined, then connections from service A will start waiting for service B to respond. The request processing threads in the pool exhausts and will crash. Here we need to make sure that the service fails quickly, and avoids escalation of failures to other systems.

Circuit Breaker

The circuit breaker pattern is commonly used to ensure that when there is failure that a failed service does not adversely affect the entire system.

The basic idea behind the circuit breaker is very simple. protected function call will be wrapped in a circuit breaker object, which monitors for failures. Once the failures reach a certain threshold, the circuit breaker trips and further calls to the circuit breaker will either be denied or routed to the configured fallback method.

The following are typical cases of abnormal service behavior:

- Service is down
- Service call is taking too long
- Service call is throwing errors

Without proper mechanisms in place, errors, in particular, latencies will trickle up to the calling clients where they will potentially exhaust limited resources. When cascading failures occur, the overall system availability is significantly affected.

A circuit breaker is an always-live system keeping watch over dependency invocations. In case of a high failure rate, the circuit breaker stops the calls from going through for a small amount of time, rather than responding with a response or routing to a fallback.

4.11 Testing

Below are the common patterns used for testing Microservices.

Service Integration Contract Test

An application consists of numerous services. Services often invoke other services. Automated tests must be written to verify that a service behaves correctly. This pattern talks about writing a test suite for a service that is written by the developers of another service that consumes it. The test suite verifies that the service meets the consuming service's expectations.

This pattern has the following benefits:

- Testing a service in isolation is easier, faster, more reliable and cheap

Service Component Test

An application consists of numerous services. Services often invoke other services. Automated tests must be written to verify that a service behaves correctly. This pattern talks about using test doubles (mock data) to test a service end to end in isolation.

This pattern has the following benefits:

- Testing a service in isolation is easier, faster, more reliable and cheap

4.12 Release

Below are few patterns related to Microservices release.

Blue Green Deployment

This pattern suggests maintaining two production environments that are identical. A new release goes to one of the unused environments, say green. The switch is done from a router to send traffic to the green deployment. If successful, the green environment becomes the new production and the blue environment can be made inactive. If there is an issue, the rollback is easier. The next cycle happens in reverse, with deployment to blue environment, thus alternating between the two environments.

Semantic Versioning

This pattern gives overview of handling multiple services at the same time. In this case, both services are active, one for the legacy and one with the new changes. Based on the request, content based routing pattern can be used to switch the queue to send the request.

Canary Release

This pattern is a variant of blue green pattern used to introduce a change to a small set of users using a routing logic that selects a group of customers for new service. The redirection logic decides to whom the messages needs to be targeted to.

4.13 Summary

This chapter highlighted various patterns used in Microservices design across many phases of the development lifecycle and layers. Microservices Patterns teaches developers and architects how to build applications with the Microservice architecture rather than simply advocating for the use. As Microservices architecture implementation is relatively new, patterns are required to make sure team do not fall for common pitfalls across design, development, deployment, release and monitoring.

5. Designing Microservices System

The focus of the enterprises building the applications using Microservices is to balance the speed and safety at a scale. To balance this, we need to tune the enterprise culture, architecture, interfaces and services. Designing Microservices need a different perspective and principles to decompose domain and identify all the design elements to maximize loose coupling, cohesion and minimize inter service communication. Below sections highlight the design methodologies, principles, patterns and the process for service identification along with examples.

Microservices design model consists of service, solution, process and tools, organization and culture.

Service: Implementing well-designed Microservices and APIs are essential to a Microservice system. In a Microservice system, the services form the atomic building blocks from which the entire organism is built.

Solution: Solution architecture represents the macro view of the solution and it is distinct from the individual service design elements. When designing a particular Microservice the decisions are bounded by the need to produce a single output— the service itself. However, when designing a solution architecture, the decisions are bounded by the need to coordinate all the inputs and outputs of multiple services. This macro-level view of the system allows the designer to induce more desirable system behavior.

For example, a solution architecture that provides discovery, safety, and routing features that reduces the complexity of individual services.

Process and Tools: Choosing the right processes and tools is an important factor in producing good Microservice system behavior. For example, adopting standardized processes like DevOps and Agile or tools like Docker containers can increase the changeability of the system.

Organization: From a Microservice system perspective, organizational design includes the structure, direction of authority, granularity, and composition of teams. Many of the enterprises, that have had success with Microservice architecture point to their organizational design as a key ingredient.

Culture: culture is a set of values, beliefs, or ideals that are shared by all of the workers within an organization. Culture is important because it shapes all of the atomic decisions that people within the system will make.

Major steps of the Microservices design process are, Identification of Goals, Development of Microservices Principles, Iteration and Implementation. While these are more prominent steps to be adopted for the process, these can be tweaked based on enterprise needs.

It is a good idea to have a set of high-level goals to use as a guide when making decisions about what to do and how to go about doing it. The major goals of the Microservices design are,

- Reduce Cost: The focus is to reduce overall cost of designing, implementing, and maintaining IT services
- Increase Release Speed: The focus is to increase the speed at which the team can get from idea to deployment of services
- Improve Resilience: scope is to improve the resilience of service network
- Enable Visibility: It helps to view, what is going on in service network

5.1 Sizing of Microservices

It is important that, while designing a Microservice, there is a need to decide on the number and size of individual Microservices. There is no strict rule regarding the optimal size, but there are some practices that have been proven in real-world systems. The sizing of micro services depends on the partitioning of the problem space if it is a new development application or splitting the existing monolithic application into individual Microservices.

Microservices cannot be too large or too small. Large services are hard to work with, hard to deploy, and take longer to start and stop. On the other side, when Microservices are too small, the resource cost of deploying, inter microservices communication and operating such a service overshadows its utility.

Famously know in Amazon, "if you cannot feed the team building a microservice with two pizzas, your microservice is too big".

Microservice granularity can also be determined based on business needs. Making services too granular, or requiring too many dependencies on other Microservices, can introduce latency.

Microservices allow teams to plan, develop, and deploy features of a system in the cloud without tight coordination. It is therefore to be expected that Microservice number and size are dictated by organizational and technical principles.

5.2 Design Methodologies

One of the important challenges in design process is to decompose the domain into sub domains, identify bounded contexts and various elements of Microservices. Multiple approaches for domain decomposition are given below, we will elaborate only on first two techniques.

- Decompose by business capability and define services corresponding to business capabilities.
- Decompose by domain-driven design.
- Decompose by verb or use case and define services that are responsible for particular actions. e.g. a New License Service that's responsible for completing the issuing of New License
- Decompose by nouns or resources by defining a service that is responsible for all operations on entities/resources of a given type. e.g. an Account Service that is responsible for managing user accounts.

Decompose by business capability

Define services corresponding to business capabilities. A business capability is a concept from business architecture modeling. It is something that a business does in order to generate value. A business capability often corresponds to a business object, e.g. let's take an example from government domain

- License Request is responsible for requesting New License
- License Processing is responsible for License Processing

Business capabilities are often organized into a multi-level hierarchy. For example, an enterprise application might have top-level categories such as License, Fees, and Processing etc.

Examples

Few important business capabilities of a government domain include:

- License Management

- Fees Management
- Inspection
- Reports

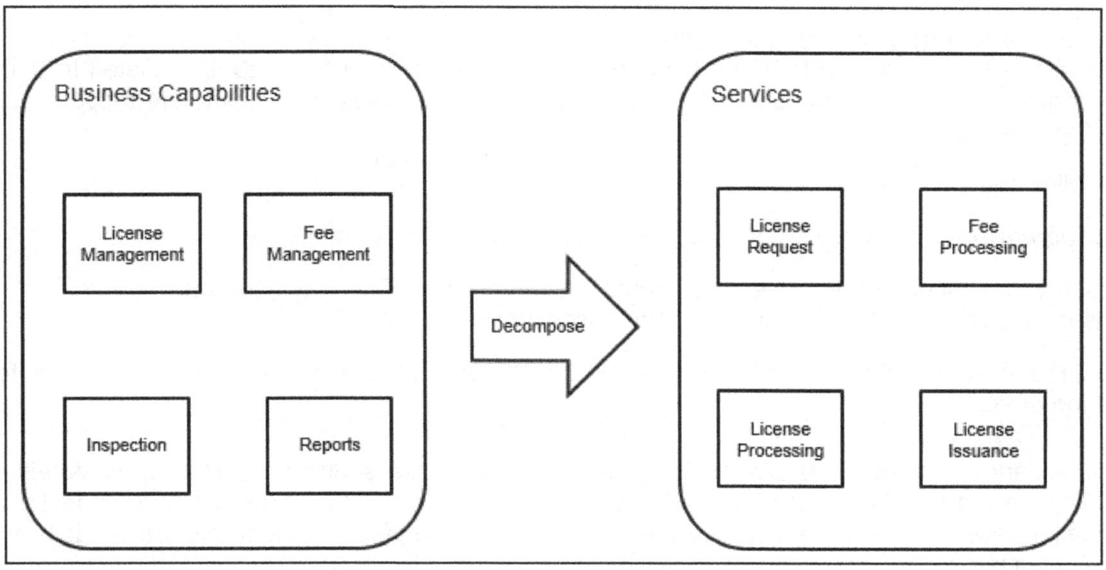

Domain decomposition by business capability

Benefits of decomposing by business capability:

- Stable architecture since the business capabilities are relatively stable
- Development teams are cross-functional, autonomous, and organized around delivering business value rather than technical features
- Services are cohesive and loosely coupled

Decompose by domain-driven design

Domain-driven design (DDD) provides a structure of practices and terminology for making design decisions that focus and accelerate software projects dealing with complex domains. Complex problem domains contain lots of information and we need to find a way to distil relevant information from the problem domain. DDD helps us to find useful and right models.

DDD refers to the application's problem space - the business - as the domain. A domain is consisting of multiple subdomains. Each subdomain corresponds to a different part of the business.

Subdomains can be classified as follows:

- Core - Key differentiator for the business and the most valuable part of the application
- Supporting – Sub domains related to what the business does but not core. These can be implemented in-house or outsourced
- Generic – Sub domains applicable/used across the enterprise. Ex: Reporting system, utility systems (like email) etc.

Following are important models to consider for DDD:

- Ubiquitous Language
- Bounded Context
- Context Map

Ubiquitous Language

The ubiquitous language is a collective language that stores all the terms and key phrases that is used by the software development team. It is one of DDD's most important models. It is not technical but related to domain created by all the team members - developers, business analysts and other professional who are responsible for the software development process.

This contains the following:

- Informal Diagrams for representing domains, sub domains and bounded contexts
- Main glossary with simple definitions and alternative terms in it. This way, the team creates its own ubiquitous language with set terms, phrases, and descriptions
- Small documents with some informal diagrams and text describing the behavior and constraints for a subset of the model

It is absolutely necessary to develop a model of the domain by having the software specialists' work with the domain experts. The developers have their minds full of classes, methods, algorithms, patterns, and tend to always make a match between a real life concept and a programming artifact. Domain experts will talk about those things in their own jargon.

Bounded Context

Enterprise projects are usually large projects, which employ various technologies and resources. The design of such projects should still be based on a domain model, and we need to take appropriate measure to ensure the success of the project. When multiple teams work on a project, code development is done in parallel, each team being assigned a specific part of the model. Those parts are not independent, but are more or less interconnected.

An enterprise project could have one model covering the entire domain of the enterprise, with no contradictions and overlapping terms. A unified enterprise model is an ideal which is not easily accomplished, and sometimes it is not even worth trying it. The solution is not so obvious, because it is the opposite of all we have learned so far. Instead of trying to keep one big model that will fall apart later, we should consciously divide it into several models. Several models well integrated can evolve independently as long as they obey the contract they are bound to. Each model should have a clearly delimited border, and the relationships between models should be defined with precision.

When we work on a large enterprise application, we need to define the context for each model we create. Each model has a context. When we deal with a single model, the context is implicit. We do not need to define it. A model should be small enough to be assigned to one team.

The context of a model is the set of conditions which need to be applied to make sure that the terms used in the model have a specific meaning. The main idea is to define the scope of a model, to draw up the boundaries of its context, then do the most possible to keep the model unified. It is hard to keep a model pure when it spans the entire enterprise project, but it is much easier when it is limited to a specified area. Explicitly define the context within which a model applies. Explicitly set boundaries in terms of team organization, usage within specific parts of the application, and physical manifestations such as code bases and database schemas. Keep the model strictly consistent within these bounds.

A Bounded Context is not a Module. A Bounded Context provides the logical frame inside of which the model evolves. Modules are used to organize the elements of a model, so Bounded Context encompasses the Module.

The following section outlines the building blocks of bounded context, they represent some of the key elements of object modelling and software design from the viewpoint of domain-driven design. It is worth to note that an iterative approach to be adopted in finalizing various building blocks.

- **Entities:** There is a category of objects which seem to have an identity, which remains the same throughout the states of the software. For these objects it is not the attributes which matter, but a thread of continuity and identity, which spans the life of a system and can extend beyond it (persistent). Such objects are called Entities. Entities are accessible with an identity in an application. In fact, an entity is domain concepts with identity and continuity. Implementing entities in software means creating identity.

  Usually the identity is either an attribute of the object, a combination of attributes, an attribute specially created to preserve and express identity, or even a behaviour. It is important for two objects with different identities to be to be easily distinguished by the system, and two objects with the same identity to be considered the same by the system. Entities are important objects of a domain model, and they should be considered from the beginning of the modelling process. Below are few rules to consider for entities,

  - Entities are core domain concepts
  - Should be distinguishable with identity rather than attributes ex: License, each license with different licenseID will be treated as different license.
  - Should not have a complex structure (in terms of contained elements)
  - Mutable
  - License, inspection, Issue, Citizen, LicenseRequest etc. are examples of entities.

- **Value Objects:** An object that is used to describe descriptive aspects of a domain, and which does not have conceptual identity, is named Value Object. Value objects are accessible by their value rather than their identity. They are Identity-less, immutable and highly cohesive. Their values don't change (or change rarely) and have no life cycle. It is highly recommended that value objects be immutable. Value objects are Combinable. This means the values of the two can be combined. As value objects are immutable, the result will be a new value object with the desired value. The original objects remain unchanged. Below are few rules to consider for value objects,

  - Value objects should be made immutable
  - Value Objects should be kept thin and simple.
  - When a Value Object is needed by another party, it can be simply passed by value
  - Value Objects can contain other Value Objects, and they can even contain references to Entities
  - Attributes chosen to make up a Value Object should form a conceptual whole (cohesive)
  - Fee, Status, Report etc. are examples of value objects.

- **Aggregates:** Aggregate is a pattern used to define object ownership and boundaries. A model can contain a large number of domain objects. No matter how much consideration we put in the design, it happens that many objects are associated with one another, creating a complex net of relationships. There are several types of associations. For every traversable association in the model, there has to be corresponding software mechanism which enforces it. Real associations between domain object end up in the code, and many times even in the database.

  An Aggregate is a group of associated objects which are considered as one unit with regard to data changes. The Aggregate is demarcated by a boundary which separates the objects inside from those outside. Each Aggregate has one root. The root is an Entity, and it is the only object accessible from outside. The root can hold references to any of the aggregate objects, and the other objects can hold references to each other, but an outside object can hold references only to the root object. If there are other Entities inside the boundary, the identity of those entities is local, making sense only inside the aggregate.

  Below are few rules to consider while designing aggregates:

  - Objects inside an Aggregate should be allowed to hold references to roots of other aggregates.

- The root Entity has global identity, and is responsible for maintaining the invariants. Internal Entities have local identity.
- Cluster the Entities and Value Objects into Aggregates and define boundaries around each.
- Choose one Entity to be the root of each Aggregate, and control all access to the objects inside the boundary through the root.
- Allow external objects to hold references to the root only.
- Aggregates referencing other aggregates should use their global identity rather than their references
- Transactions should not cross aggregate boundaries.
- Design small aggregates. Limit the Aggregate to just the Root Entity and a minimal number of attributes and/or Value objects. But, this definition depends on the requirement and scenario.

LicenseService,ReportService, InspcetionService are example of aggregates. These services are referred with suffix "Aggregate" in the design realization chapter.

- **Factories:** Entities and Aggregates can often be large and complex – too complex to create in the constructor of the root entity. When the object construction is a laborious process, creating the object involves a lot of knowledge about the internal structure of the object, about the relationships between the objects contained, and the rules applied to them. This means that each client of the object will hold specific knowledge about the object built. This breaks encapsulation of the domain objects and of the Aggregates.

  Factories are used to encapsulate the knowledge necessary for object creation, and they are especially useful to create Aggregates. When the root of the Aggregate is created, all the objects contained by the Aggregate are created along with it, and all the invariants are enforced. It is important for the creation process to be atomic.

  There are times when a Factory is needed. Use a factory when,

  - The construction of an object is complicated.
  - The creation of an object involves the creation of others objects.
  - The class is the type and hierarchy involved, so need to choose between a list of concrete implementations.

- **Repositories:** The purpose of repository is to encapsulate all the logic needed to obtain object references. The domain objects won't have to deal with the infrastructure to get the needed references to other objects of the domain. They will just get them from the Repository and the model is regaining its clarity and focus. The Repository may store references to some of the objects. When an object is created, it may be saved in the Repository, and retrieved from there to be used later. If the client requested an object from the Repository, and the Repository does not have it, it may get it from the storage.

  Repository acts as a storage place for globally accessible objects. The overall effect is that the domain model is decoupled from the need of storing objects or their references, and accessing the underlying persistence infrastructure. A Repository should have a set of methods used to retrieve objects. The client calls such a method and passes one or more parameters which represent the selection criteria used to select an object or a set of matching objects.

- **Services:** When we analyze the domain and try to define the main objects that make up the model, we discover that some aspects of the domain are not easily mapped to objects. Key concepts of the domain are introduced in the language, and the nouns of the language are easily mapped to objects. The verbs of the language, associated with their corresponding nouns become the part of the behaviour of those objects. But there are some actions in the domain, some verbs, which do not seem to belong to any object. They represent an important behaviour of the domain, so they cannot be neglected or simply incorporated into some of the Entities or Value Objects. When such a behaviour is recognized in the domain, the best practice is to declare it as a Service. Such an object does not have an internal state, and its purpose is to simply provide functionality for the domain.

There are three characteristics of a Service:

- The operation performed by the Service refers to a domain concept which does not naturally belong to an Entity or Value Object.
- The operation performed refers to other objects in the domain.
- The operation is stateless.

There are three different service types:

- **Edge/API Services:** API services are exposed either on the edge server or on API Gateway. They expose client specific API and can also act as coarse-grained services to orchestrate across multiple Microservices within or across bounded contexts. These services can interact with composite services or directly with core services.

  API services can also communicate with the enterprise integration infrastructure (typically ESB/MOM) to access any enterprise application on premise

- **Composite Services:** Composite services orchestrate across multiple core services. These services will be communicating with the other services using the event-sourcing model or other means like orchestration. These services are identified in design realization.

- **Core services:** These services are the basic building blocks for Microservices architecture. These services encapsulate an entity or an aggregate (fine grained) within a given bounded context. Best practice says that the granularity of the Microservices must be fine grained. These services are identified in design realization.

- **Data Stores:** These are the data stores associated with each Microservice. Ideally a Microservice should have its own data store. This data store can be specific to requirement like RDBMS, NoSQL, Graph etc. The approach of selecting data stores according to the characteristics of each data type is polyglot persistence. The other model is multi-model databases. It is an alternative or complement to the polyglot persistence approach. Model is the primary abstraction provided by a data store, such as tabular (both relational and non-relational), column store, key-value, document, or graph. Multi-model application as one that uses more than one type of data store, while a multi-model database is one that supports more than one abstraction. Each model has pros and cons and these needs to be considered before choosing a model.

Below diagram shows how these services hierarchically relate to each other,

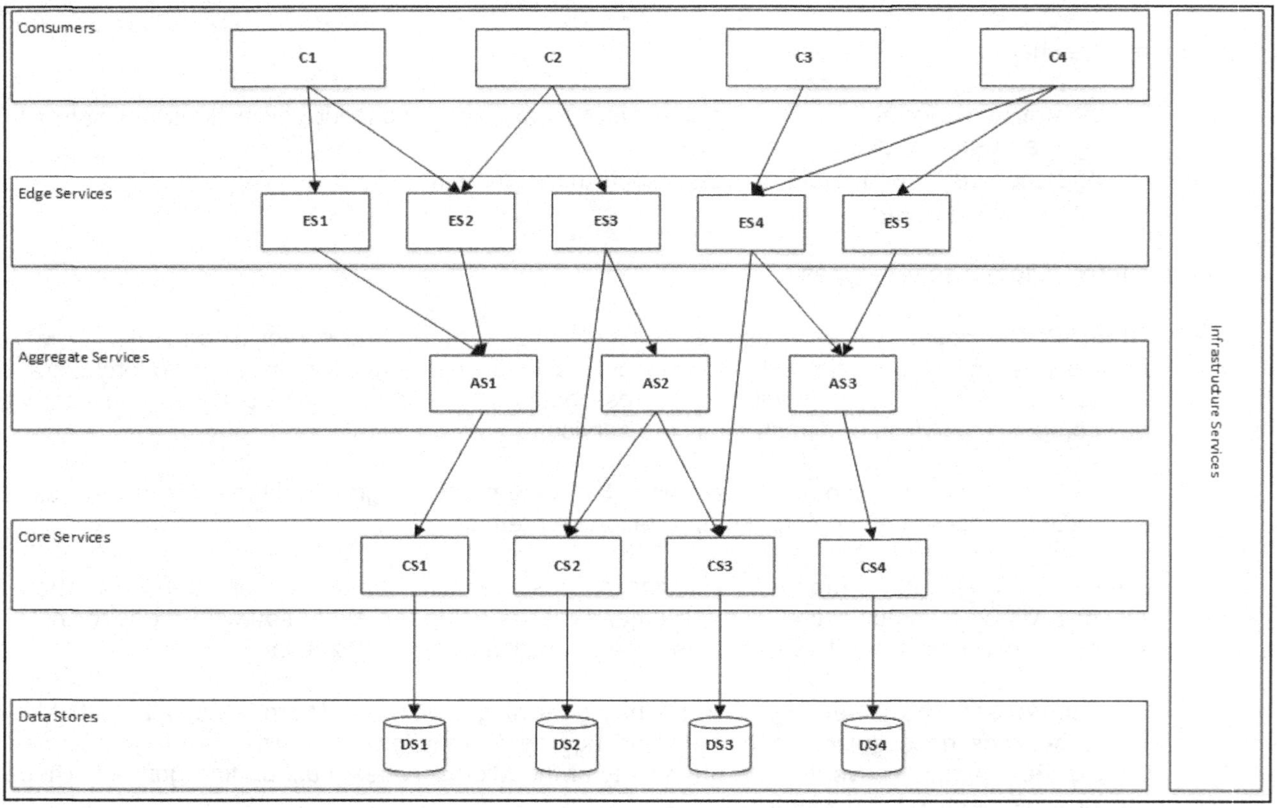

Microservices Hierarchy

Context Map

An enterprise application has multiple models, and each model has its own Bounded Context. It is advisable to use the context as the basis for team organization. People in the same team can communicate more easily, and they can do a better job integrating the model and the implementation. While every team works on its model, it is good for everyone to have an idea of the overall picture.

A Context Map is a document which outlines the different Bounded Contexts and the relationships between them. A Context Map can be a diagram like the one below, or it can be any written document. The level of detail may vary. What it is important is that everyone working on the project shares and understands it. Below diagram represents the context map for License Management System. For illustration purpose few bounded contexts were considered.

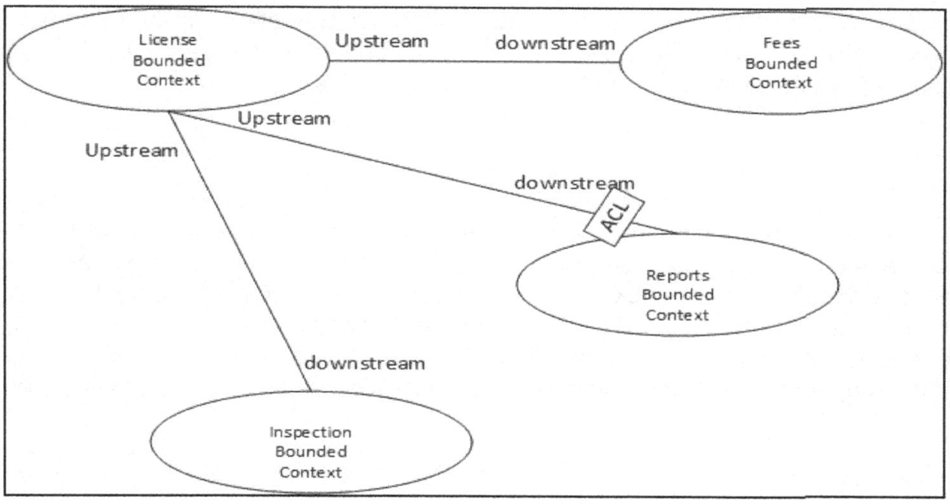

Context Map

It's not enough to have separate unified models. They have to be integrated, because each model's functionality is just a part of the entire system. In the end the pieces have to be assembled together, and the entire system must work properly. Each Bounded Context should have a name. That helps the team communication a lot when talking about the entire system. Everyone should know the boundaries of each context and the mapping between contexts and code.

A common practice is to define the contexts, then create modules for each context, and use a naming convention to indicate the context each module belongs to. A series of patterns which can be used to create Context Maps where contexts have clear roles and their relationships are pointed out in following section. The shared Kernel and Customer-Supplier are patterns with a high degree of interaction between contexts. Separate Ways is a pattern used when we want the contexts to be highly independent and evolve separately.

There are another two patterns dealing with the interaction between a system and a legacy system or an external one, and they are Open Host Services and Anticorruption Layers.

Anticorruption Layer: When management and communication models are inconsistent with SHARED KERNEL, PARTNERSHIP or CUSTOMER-SUPPLIER DEVELOPMENT, the translation procedure is complex. The downstream client should create so-called anticorruption layer to match up his or her system with the upstream system in terms that are used in his or her domain's model. This layer corresponds with the other system using the current interface without having to modify the system.

Open Host Service: In this case, we identify an open host service that provides access to the system as if it was a set of multiple services. In case there are new integration requirements, the host service can be expanded or specified.

5.3 Microservices Design Principles

Principles offer more concrete guidance on how to act in order to achieve goals. Principles are not rules, they do not set out required elements. Instead, they offer examples on how to act in identifiable situations. Principles can also be used to inform best practices. Many of the organizations will have their own set of principles within their company.

The following are the major Principles need to be adopted during Microservices design process.

Lightweight

Microservices have to be lightweight in order to facilitate smaller memory footprints and faster start up times. This facilitates faster MTTR, allows for services to be deployed on smaller runtimes instances, hence horizontally scaling better. As compared to heavy runtime times such as Application Servers, smaller runtimes such as Tomcat, netty, node.js and undertow are more suited. Also, the Services should exchange data in lightweight text formats such as JSON or binary formats such as Avro, Thrift or Protocol Buffers.

Reactive

This is applicable for services with highly concurrent loads or slightly longer response times. Typical server implementations block thread to execute imperative programming styles. As Microservices could depend on other Microservices or I/O resources like database, blocking threads could increase Operating system overheads. Reactive style operates on non-blocking I/o, uses call back handlers and reacts to events. This is does not block threads and as result increases the scalability and load handling characteristics of the Microservices much better. Database drivers have started supporting reactive paradigms, e.g. Mongo DB reactive streams java driver.

Stateless

Stateless services scale better and start faster as there is no state to be passivated on shutdown or activated on start up. They are also more resilient, as termination of service will not result in loss of data. Being stateless is also a step towards being lightweight. If state is required, a service can delegate state storage to high speed persistent (key value store), or hold it in distributed caches.

Atomic

This is the core design principle of Microservices. They should be easy to change, test and deploy. All these can be achieved if the services are reasonably small and do the smallest business unit of work that can be done independently. If there is low coupling, the services will be easier to modify and independently deploy. Composite Microservices may be required on need basis, but should be limited in design.

Externalized Configuration

Typical application properties and configurations were traditionally managed as configuration files. Given the multiple and large deployment of Microservices, this practice will start getting cumbersome, as scale of the services increase. Hence it is better to externalize the configurations in the config server, so that it can be maintained in hierarchical structure per environment. Features such as hot changes can also be easier to reflect many services at once.

Consistent

Services should be written in a consistent style as per the coding standards and naming convention guidelines. Common concerns such as serialization, REST, exception handling, logging, configuration & property access, metering, monitoring, provisioning, validations, data access should be consistently done through reusable assets, annotations, etc. it should be easier for another developer from same team to understand the intent and operation of the service.

Resilient

Service should handle exceptions arising from technical reasons (connectivity, runtime), and business reasons (invalid inputs) and not crash. They should use patterns like timeouts and circuit breaker to ensure that the failures are handled carefully.

Service Statistics

Report their usage statistics, number of times accessed, average response time, etc. via JMX API, and/or publish it via libraries to central monitoring infrastructures. Log audit, error, business events in the standards prescribed. Expose their condition via health check interfaces, e.g. as done by spring Actuator.

Versioned

Microservices may need to support multiple versions for different clients, till all clients migrate to higher versions. Hence the deployments and URL should support semantic versioning. i.e. X.x.x

Smaller

The notion of work-unit granularity is a crucial one in many contexts of modern software development. Whether defined explicitly or implicitly, we can clearly see the trend showing up in such foundational methodologies as Agile Development, Lean Startup, and Continuous Delivery, among others. These methodologies have revolutionized project management, product development, and DevOps, respectively. It is interesting to note that each one of them has the principle of size reduction at its core: reducing the size or scope of the problem, reducing the time it takes to complete a task, reducing the time it takes to get feedback, and reducing the size of the deployment unit.

API Design for Microservices

When considering Microservice component boundaries, the source code itself is only part of our concern. Microservice components only become valuable when they can communicate with other components in the system. They each have an interface or API. Just as we need to achieve a high level of separation, independence, and modularity of our code we need to make sure that our APIs, the component interfaces, are also loosely coupled. Otherwise, we won't be able to deploy two Microservices independently, which is one of our primary goals in order to balance speed and safety.

Message-Oriented

Just as we work to write component code that can be safely refactored over time, we need to apply the same efforts to the shared interfaces between components. The most effective way to do this is to adopt a message-oriented implementation for Microservice APIs. The notion of messaging as a way to share information between components dates back to the initial ideas about how object-oriented programming would work.

Messaging is a key design practice. For example, Netflix relies on message formats like Avro, Protobuf, and Thrift over TCP/IP for communicating internally and JSON over HTTP for communicating to external consumers (e.g., mobile phones, browsers, etc.). By adopting a message-oriented approach, developers can expose general entry points into a component (e.g., an IP address and port number) and receive task-specific messages at the same time. This allows for changes in message content as a way of refactoring components safely over time. The key lesson learned here is that for far too long, developers have viewed APIs and web services as tools to transmit serialized "objects" over the wire. However, a more efficient approach is to look at a complex system as a collection of services exchanging messages over a wire.

Capability Centric Design

As software engineers, we have been trained to think in terms of data, first and foremost. To give the simplest example, it has pretty much been ingrained in our memory is, to start system design by first designing the relevant data models. When asked to build an application, the very first task most software engineers will complete is identifying entities and designing database tables for data storage. This is an efficient way of designing centralized systems and whole generations of programmers have been trained to think this way. But data-centric design is not a good way to implement distributed systems—especially systems that rely on independently deployable Microservices. The biggest reason for this is the absence of strong, centralized, uniform control over the entire system in the case of distributed systems, which makes a formerly efficient process inefficient.

The first step in breaking the data-centric habit is to rethink our system designs. We need to stop designing systems as a collection of data services and instead use business capabilities as the design element. It turns out that capabilities-centric design is more suitable for Microservices than a more traditional, data-centric design.

Event Sourcing

We've mentioned that there are some deep-rooted software engineering habits that greatly affect the way we typically approach systems engineering. One of the most widespread of those habits is structural data modeling. It has become very natural for us to describe models as collections of interacting logical entities and then to map those logical entities to physical tables where the data is stored. More recently, we have started using NoSQL and object stores that take us slightly away from the relational world, but in essence the approach is still the same: we design structural entities that model objects around us and then we save the object's state in a database store of some kind. Whether storage happens in table rows and columns, serialized as JSON strings, or as object graphs, we are still performing CRUD-based modelling. But this is not the only way to model the world. Instead of storing structures that model the state of our world, we can store events that lead to the current state of our world. This modelling approach is called event sourcing. Event sourcing is all about storing facts and any time and have state (structural models). In this context, facts mean the descriptive value of an event occurrence. An example could be "a license has been adjudicated and is sent for payment".

We need one more design pattern, CQRS, to complement event sourcing toward being able to design effective data storage for Microservices with data persistence models that can avoid data sharing at even very small Microservice sizes.

Distributed Transactions – Saga

The shared data model is not the only use case that can introduce tight coupling between Microservices. Another important threat is workflows. A lot of real-life processes cannot be represented with a single, atomic operation, since they are a sequence of steps. When we are dealing with such workflows, the result only makes sense if all of the steps can be executed. In other words, if any step in the sequence fails, the resulting state of the relevant system becomes invalid. We probably recognize this problem from RDBMS systems where we call such processes "transactions." However, database transactions are local, contained within the confines of a single database where their implementations predominantly rely on the use of a shared state (i.e., we put locks on the rows and tables that participate in a transaction, guaranteeing data consistency). Once the transaction is fully executed we can remove the locks, or if any step of the transaction steps fails, we can roll back the steps already attempted.

For distributed workflows and share-nothing environments (and Microservice architecture is both of those), we cannot use traditional transaction implementations with data locks and ACID compliance, since such transactions require shared data and local execution. This is where Saga fits. A saga is a sequence of local transactions. Each local transaction updates the database and publishes a message or event to trigger the next local transaction in the saga. If a local transaction fails because it violates a business rule, then the saga executes a series of compensating transactions that undo the changes that were made by the preceding local transactions. Due to its highly fault-tolerant, distributed nature, Sagas are very well-suited to replace traditional transactions when transactions across Microservice boundaries are required in a Microservice

5.4 Factors Applied to Microservices

In the modern era, software is commonly delivered as a service: called web apps, or software-as-a-service. The twelve-factor app is a methodology for building cloud native applications that:

- Use declarative formats for setup automation, to minimize time and cost for new developers joining the project;
- Have a clean contract with the underlying operating system, offering maximum portability between execution environments;
- Are suitable for deployment on modern cloud platforms, obviating the need for servers and systems administration;
- Minimize divergence between development and production, enabling continuous deployment for maximum agility;
- And can scale up without significant changes to tooling, architecture, or development practices.

This chapter focuses on twelve factors and the recommendations for each factor. A sample questionnaire provided at the end of each factor, these will help to understand the level of maturity or current setup (information) for a particular factor, and highlights areas that may need more attention.

Technical Debt

1. Is Architecture decisions have been done: ex: ATAM, Build vs Buy
2. Is Identification of Reusable components in place
3. Is architecture addresses all the NFR's realization
4. Is architecture addresses all the critical functional realization
5. Is architecture covers all the views: Business, application, data, technology, security, integration
6. Is Standard guidelines for the usage of tools and technologies are defined
7. Is technical debt (lack of unit tests, legacy code, etc.) identified and a system to reduce it in place?
8. Systems are architected with continuous deployment in mind, supporting patterns such as dark launching to decouple deployment from release
9. What is the system for managing database changes? How are database changes linked to application changes?
10. What is the current branching/code isolation practice? Is it understood and enforced? How is merging managed? Do defects arise as a result of integration?

Codebase

One codebase per service, tracked in revision control; many deploys

The Twelve-Factor App recommends one codebase per app. In Microservices architecture, the correct approach is actually one codebase per service. Additionally, we strongly recommend the use of Git as a repository, because of its rich feature set and enormous ecosystem. While GitHub has become the default Git hosting platform in the open source community, there are many other excellent Git hosting options, depending on the organization needs.

Questions:

1. What is the Version control tool used for the code base
2. Are code reviews performed? Required? How is the code review process managed
3. Is tracking of the code up to date
4. Is code base sits on Central Repository
5. Is repository accessible to entire team

Dependencies

Explicitly declare and isolate dependencies

Twelve-Factor App suggests regardless of what platform the application is running on, use the dependency manager included with language or framework. How to install operating system or platform dependencies depends on the platform,

Use a configuration management tool (Chef, Puppet, Ansible) in non-containerized environments, to iinstall system dependencies. Do this in the Dockerfile or equivalent In a containerized environment.

Questions:

1. Is dependencies identification is done.
2. What level of dependencies are identified: Inter module, version, third party or any other.
3. Is all dependencies are controllable and managed to minimum

Config

Store configuration in the environment

Anything that changes between deployments is configuration. The Twelve-Factor App guidelines recommend storing all configuration in the environment, rather than committing it to the repository. Following specific practices are recommended:

- Use non-version-controlled .env files for local development. Docker supports the loading of these files at runtime.
- Keep all .env files in a secure storage system, such as Vault, to make the files available to the development teams, but not committed to Git.
- Use an environment variable for anything that can change at runtime, and for any secrets that should not be committed to the shared repository.
- Once application is deployed to a delivery platform, use the delivery platform's mechanism for managing environment variables

Questions:

1. Are application and infrastructure configurations externalized from the applications
2. Is defined application frameworks are capable of refresh configuration without application downtime
3. Is configurable items are hardcoded, ex: credentials, API keys in code level.
4. Is pre-defined files or environment level are set up, such that code can read from there in tern that to prevent application being in risk from production data leaks and production errors.

Backing Services

Treat backing services as attached resources

Backing service is "Any service the application consumes over the network as part of its normal operation".

The implication for Microservices is that anything external to a service is treated as an attached resource, including other services. This ensures that every service is completely portable and loosely coupled with the other resources in the system. Additionally, separation increases flexibility during development – developers only need to run the services they are modifying, not others.

Questions:

1. Is application design handles backing services, such that update should occur without any code changes.
2. Is backing service details are stored configuration files

Build, Release, Run

Strictly separate build and run stages

To support strict separation of build, release, and run stages, as recommended by the Twelve-Factor App, we recommend the use of a continuous integration/ continuous delivery (CI/CD) tool to automate builds. Docker images make it easy to separate the build and run stages.

Questions:

1. What is the current build process? Is continuous integration used? What technology is in place to manage builds?
2. Is build and deployment are treated as two different stages from each other
3. What steps are adopted in build deployment process?
    a. Code promotion process
4. How often are releases, both major and minor, deployed to the various environments?
5. How are database changes built and deployed?
6. What type of automation tools are used in build process?
7. How are the current deployment environments configured? How closely do the testing and staging environments mimic the production environment?

Processes

Execute the app in one or more stateless processes

Important point is that application needs to be stateless. This makes it easy to scale a service horizontally by simply adding more instances of that service. Store any stateful data, or data that needs to be shared between instances, in a backing service such as Redis.

Questions:

1. Is data stored outside the running code?
    a. It is recommended storing data outside of running code in order to prevent issues while scale up.

Data Isolation

Each service manages its own data

Recommend that access to the persistent data owned by a service allowed only via the service's API. This prevents implicit service contracts between Microservices and ensures that Microservices can't become tightly coupled. Data isolation also allows the developer to choose, for each service, the type of data store that best suits its needs (polyglot persistence).

Questions:

1. Is export services done via port binding?

Concurrency

Scale out via the process model

The Unix process model is a predecessor to microservices architecture, as it allows specialization and resource sharing for different tasks within a monolithic application. In a microservices architecture, each service can independently scale horizontally, to the extent supported by the underlying infrastructure. With containerized services, further get the concurrency is achieved.

Questions:

1. Is there any process model used to scale out application
    a. Each process should be stateless and able to scale, restart, or clone itself when needed. This approach will improve the sustainability and scalability of application as a whole.

Disposability

Maximize robustness with fast startup and graceful shutdown

Instances of a service need to be disposable so they can be started, stopped, and redeployed quickly, and with no loss of data. Services deployed in Docker containers satisfy this requirement automatically, as it is an inherent feature of containers. Storing state or session data in queues or other backing services ensures that a request is handled seamlessly in the event of a container crash.

Questions:

1. Is applications design (keeping processes stateless and store the state in backing services) covers fast startup and graceful shutdown.

Dev/Prod Parity

Keep development, staging, and production as similar as possible

Keep all environments – development, staging, production, and so on – as identical as possible, to reduce the risk that bugs show up only in some environments.

Questions:

1. How are deployments to testing, staging and production managed? Is there an automated framework in place to manage deployments?
2. What type of environments are used for Development, pre-production and production
    a. Development, pre-production and production environments are as similar as possible.
    b. Is infrastructure stack, config management processes, software and runtime versions and deployment tools are the same everywhere.
3. What mechanisms are in place to monitor and alert on production systems? How are the metrics Mean Time to Detect (MTTD) and Mean Time to Recovery (MTTR) measured and recorded?
4. What is the current disaster recovery plan? Does the plan account for all development and production environments?
5. How is capacity measured? Is there a system in place to automatically adjust resources to handle additional demand?

Logs

Treat logs as event streams

Instead of including code in a microservice for routing or storing logs, use one of the many good log-management solutions on the market. Further, deciding how to work with logs needs to be part of a larger APM and/or PaaS strategy.

Questions:

1. Are there any control mechanisms for access of logs
2. Is Standard Mechanism for the application logging defined?
    a. Logs are continuous stream that is captured and stored by a separate service.

Admin Processes

Run admin and management tasks as one-off processes

In a production environment, run administrative and maintenance tasks separately from the app. Containers make this very easy, as a container can be spin up very quickly to run a task and then shut it down.

Questions:
1. Is admin job run as a process
2. What activities are performed using admin process
    a. Data collection jobs that are used to gather key information about application. This information will be needed to assess the state of production environment

Cloud Computing
1. What is organisation policy for using the public cloud?
2. Is the application infrastructure self-service
3. Is the infrastructure elastic
4. Are any platform PaaS services in use?
5. Which PaaS are in use
6. When a dev team wants more infrastructure, what do they do?
7. When a dev team wants to update a release, what do they do?
8. Is the decisions about application hosting is done?

IDM & Security
1. Is source repository, artifact repositories configured with an IDM
2. Are access policies defined for source code
3. What is enterprise policy towards security of your source code
4. How granular is enterprise access control to artefacts

Artifact Repository
1. Is there an artefact repository in place
2. How are application dependencies and artefact versioning handled during build lifecycle
3. Any dependency visualizations tools integrated into the pipeline
4. How does developer compare multiple built artefacts

Data Security and Governance

1. How do we secure production Data
2. Are developers allowed to view production data
3. Data sensitivity issues

Backup and Archival

1. How are accidental / deliberate deletions to source code and artefacts handled
2. Do you have any backup and archival solutions in place
3. What is your application retirement strategy

DevOps Portal, Workflows and lifecycle Management

1. Do you have any portals to monitor application lifecycle states
2. Are all the processes defined and documented in the portal
3. Dashboards for applications
4. How robust is artefacts tracking workflow
5. Is enterprise Portal thoroughly integrated with your build and deploy lifecycle systems

Integration between Dev & Ops

1. How is a traceability achieved from a requirement to productionizing the requirement
2. How is a bug traced to a feature to a fix
3. How is change request traced
4. Is RCA integrated into the DevOps lifecycle

Rollback Automation

1. How is deployment failure in production handled
2. Is downgrading a feature / application automated
3. Upgrade and downgrade testing is done part of your automation

Test Automation

1. Are the test automation framework integrated with the continuous integration systems
2. Are there any standard test automation frameworks used
3. Is unit, component, integration and application testing automated
4. How is a feature, bug or CR accepted for production – gating criteria
5. How many test suites are present for each application
6. What categories of test suites – load, performance, security, scalability, availability

Infrastructure

1. Is infrastructure provisioning automated?
2. Is there a way to track the resource consumption

Application Retirement

1. Is there a policy defined to retire an application
2. What happens to the source code of a decommissioned application
3. What is the organizational data retention policy

Database as Code

1. Are databases changes part of DevOps lifecycle
2. How is database schema changes rolled into production
3. What kind of policies and processes are in place for changes to the database

Tracing Frameworks

1. Is any tracing frameworks used to build applications

Messaging and Monitoring Systems Integration

1. How are the developers alerted regarding failures
2. Is messaging systems integrated with build systems

Development Environments

1. Is Dev Environment provisioning automated
2. How is the devops tool chain integrated into the Development environment

5.5 Design Realization

In this section the design concepts discussed so far will be applied and realized on the LMS case study.

For simplicity we will take license domain and one process license issuance.

Below is the flow for new License issuing process. This will enable smooth and transparent issuing of licenses/ permits/ registrations quickly.

The applicant logs into the LMS system. Applicant initiates the process and shall apply for new the license/ registration/ permit required. Once the desired application is prepared and submitted to the licensing staff, the required enclosures/ documents are verified in Certificate Repository System (CR). If the documents are available, system will automatically fetch the enclosures/ documents and are shown to the applicant for the confirmation. The applicant will upload the remaining necessary documents required for the particular service and the final application is submitted for the processing. The submitted application and documents are verified by the licensing staff and tracking number is issued. The licensing staff will associate multiple licenses/ permits with single license/ permits. If the particular service requires an inspection, which is then forwarded or remarks are given as per the guidelines or policies for further processing. If the particular service requires field inspection, the inspector will view the list of licenses/ permits and inspection is done accordingly. The inspection report is generated and then forwarded to the approving authority. As per the generated report/ remarks/ recommendations given by the licensing staff/ inspector the approving authority will verify the application. The application is approved/ rejected as per the norms/ criteria.

Once the application is approved the applicant will be given status, payment details with tracking number. The applicant will log into the system check with status and make the payment. Application pays the fees as per the service and once the payment is cleared the receipt is sent through email. The new license/ permit is issued to the applicant. If the application is rejected the applicant will be updated with the reasons for rejection.

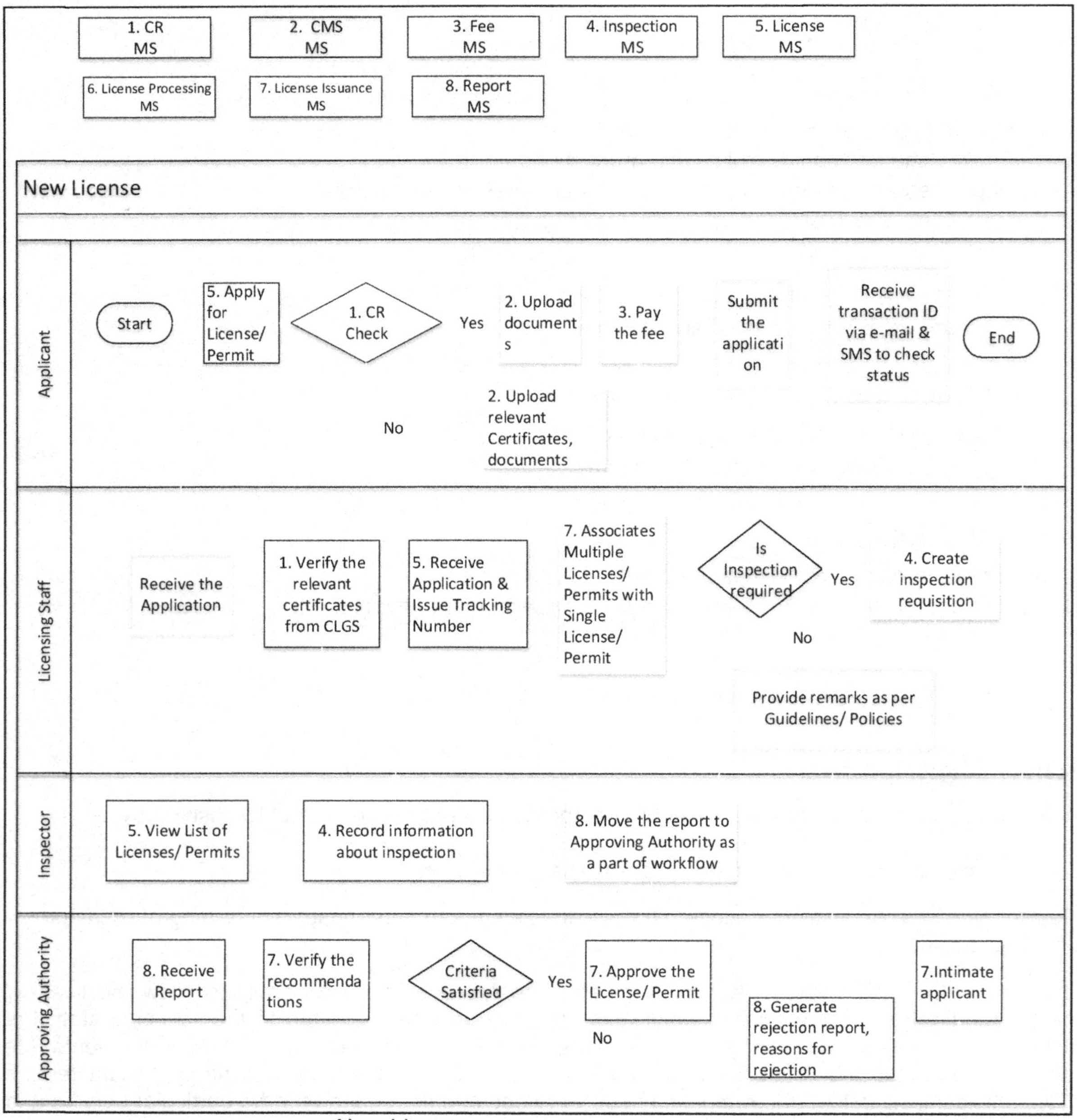

New License process

We identified various Microservices (see the legend in the above the diagram) across various bounded contexts. We will categorize the Microservices (like core Microservices, aggregate Microservices) in the chapter 6 (development of Microservices).

Below tables specify the core and aggregate (composite) Microsevices from the above process.

Core Services

Sno	Core Service Name	Bounded Context	Task (from Business Process)
1	LicenseService	License	Apply For License
2	LicenseProcessingService	License	Associate Multiple Licenses
3	LicenseService	License	View List of Licenses
4	LicenseIssuanceService	License	Approve License

5	InspectionService	Inspection	Create Inspection Requisition
6	InspectionService	Inspection	Record Information about Inspection
7	FeesService	Fees	Pay the fees
8	LicenseService	License	Issue tracking number

Aggregate (Composite Services)

Sno	Composite Service Name	Bounded Context	Task (from Business Process)
1	LicenseServiceAggregate	License	New License
2	InspectionAggregate	Inspection	Inspection Required (Yes)
3	ReportAggrgate	Reports	Record Information about Inspection

We will revisit the above services in chapter 6 (developing Microservices).

5.6 Summary

Designing a Microservices application requires application of several principles, patterns, and best practices of modular design and service-oriented architectures. This chapter explained various aspects of designing Microservices.

Starting with Microservices sizing guidelines, which provide guidelines on Microservices granularity so that we don't create too fine grained or too coarse grained services. Design methodologies help the design team to understand all the concepts of the domain driven design to come up with an extensible and proper service design. It details the domain decomposition techniques, sub domains, bounded contexts, building blocks of bounded context, rules for identifying the building block and examples to guide the designers.

Design principles guides the designer to make appropriate decision during the design of Microservices. These principles cover various characteristics that Microservices need to inherit and possess. Twelve-Factors guide the development of cloud native application in terms of code base, configuration backing services etc.

To conclude, for an extensible and scalable service design designer follows design methodology, principles and factors.

6. Development of Microservices

Similar to the software development life cycle (SDLC), it is important to understand the aspects of the Microservice development life cycle processes. This chapter discusses the lifecycle, platforms/frameworks and processes required for a successful implementation of the Microservices architecture development.

For an enterprise, Microservices adoption can be a radical departure from the current setup. It's also a cultural shift in terms of how the teams come out of the legacy way of thinking and development of applications. It is going from a "Project" mode to a "Product" mode.

Microservices can be developed in different technologies and typical will be hosted on cloud environment as cloud native application. Build and deployment follows Continuous Integration (CI) technique to enable the enterprises react to the fast changing business needs of the market by quickly developing and deploying the services. Below sections, highlight what are the challenges for enterprise in Microservices adoption, various phases and processes in development, best practices, pre requisites and tooling.

6.1 Microservice Adoption Challenges

Below are few challenges for Microservices adoption. We will look into these before introducing various concepts/aspects of development.

- Upfront investment for the enterprise in both time and money
- Transition from current technologies to new technologies
- Shift in development and operational paradigm
- Coming up with a roadmap for the enterprise
- Training the employees to have confidence and knowledge of the new development and operations models
- Architectural maturity of the enterprise to adopt Microservices
- Hard to debug, troubleshoot and monitor Microservices as they are distributed
- Transition to the product culture from the current project culture

6.2 DEVELOPMENT

Source Control

- Each service should have its own repository. This keeps checkouts small, source control logs clean and enables granular access control. Services should not be deployed together and collocating their code either.
- Standardize on a source control technology. This will keep things simple for the teams and make continuous integration and continuous delivery efforts easier.

Service Chassis

When application development has started, significant amount of time spent on putting in place the mechanisms to handle crosscutting concerns. Examples of crosscutting concern include:

1. Externalized configuration - includes credentials, and network locations of external services such as databases and message brokers
2. Logging - configuring of a logging framework such as log4j or log back
3. Health checks - a url that a monitoring service can "ping" to determine the health of the application
4. Metrics - measurements that provide insight into what the application is doing and how it is performing
5. Distributed tracing - instrument services with code that assigns each external request a unique identifier that passed between services.

6. Boilerplate code - Applications that use infrastructure services such as databases or a message brokers require boilerplate configuration/code in order to do that.

Build Microservices using a Microservice chassis framework, which handles crosscutting concerns. Few tools for service chassis are Spring Boot, drop wizard etc.

Development Environments

Developers need to be able to work quickly on their machines. To ensure a consistent environment on any operating system, the development environments be packaged as virtual machines. However, given the complexity and number of services involved in a Microservice approach, it may not be practical to bring everything up on a single developer machine. In that case, the service that is developed and running locally combined with a different integrating environment running in the cloud. The developer would be able to quickly iterate in their development environment while testing against other services running in the cloud.

Continuous Integration

Integrate working code to the mainline branch as soon as possible. Updates to the mainline branch should trigger automated builds on the continuous integration system. The builds should trigger automated tests to verify that the build is in a good shape or not.

Since these automated tests are not running on the developer's machine, it becomes feasible to run more complex and time-consuming tests on the continuous integration system. If all the tests pass, the continuous integration system should release the deployment package to the automated deployment system. Below are benefits:

- With code integrated quickly, everybody has visibility of changes made. Any conflicts created because of multiple people changing the same code shall be identified quickly and are resolved sooner.
- With full tests running often, bugs identified sooner.
- When there are few changes per iteration of integration, one can be much more confident of the correctness of those changes.

Continuous integration speeds up team's ability to deliver quality software.

Continuous Delivery

- The goal of continuous delivery is to release smaller sets of changes faster. Rather than tackle a large piece of work in one go, break it down into smaller chunks that can be completed and released one after another. Need to keep the system in a working state along the way.
- Small releases are great. They are easy to test. They simplify code review efforts. It is much easier to confidently release and deploy small sets of changes.
- To pull off continuous delivery, build, test and development cycles rapidly run through. Need to build solid continuous integration and automated deployment pipelines.

Shared Libraries

Challenge with shared libraries is that there is little control of when updates deployed across the services. It could take time before other teams deploy the updated library. In an environment where services are independently developed and deployed, any change that requires all services be simultaneously updated is not practical.

Coordinate with the service teams to ensure the updates applied in a timely manner. Shared libraries are used for managing concerns like connectivity, transport, logging and monitoring.

Service Templates

In addition to their core business logic, services need to manage a number of additional supplementary tasks. Some examples include: service registration, monitoring, client side load balancing and circuit breaking. Teams should be provided with templates which can be used to quickly bootstrap services which handle all these common tasks and integrate well into the platform.

The templates should exist to speed teams up and not to enforce structure. However, certain behaviors should be required, like those to enable registration, monitoring and logging. Should have templates available for each supported stack.

Service Replaceability

As the usage of a service grows, eventually hits the limits of architectural design. By then, should have learned enough about the specific needs and patterns of the service to be able to implement a more scalable solution. Simple and focused services is that they're also easy to replace.

As long as documented interfaces (APIs and event streams) are maintained, complete implementation can be swapped out without affecting other services. Even a change, including the API would create a new service altogether. Have any consumers of the existing service migrate over and remove the existing service when it's not being used anymore.

6.3 DEPLOYMENT

Deployment Package

A standardized deployment package is an important building block for an automated deployment pipeline.

The deployment package should have the following properties:

- **Deployed anywhere:** the same package, without changes, should be deployable to any environment. Development, testing or production.
- **External configuration/restricted data:** Configuration and restricted data shouldn't be stored within the package. Instead, they should be provided to (or retrieved by) the package at startup.
- **Isolated deployments:** If multiple services share the same resources, it's easy for a service to accidentally consume an unfair amount of resources and cause unintentional impact on other services. Isolating each deployed service minimizes such impact.

A system image fits these requirements well. A versioned system image would be created for each service. Every update to that service would result in a new image. The system image could be for a physical machine, a virtual machine or a container. When deployment package is a system image, never update a running system in place. It's just replaced by a system built from a newer image. This approach improves confidence and reliability as exact image will be tested that be deploying to production. It also avoids configuration issues as a result of direct changes to production environments.

Automated Deployment

Should have a common way to trigger automated deployments for any version of any service to any environment. Keeping deployment fully automated and simple makes it easy to confidently deploy small changes often.

If a service has to be taken down to apply an update and to avoid any disruptions, there needs a way to gracefully update a service with no downtime.

A robust approach is blue green deployment. Instances running the new version are brought up beside the original version, but serving no requests. The load balancers are then switched over to the instances running the new version (say blue), while keeping the existing version instances (say green) around for a period of time in case a quick rollback is needed. This is a powerful approach made possible on cloud environments where additional resources can be used on demand and released.

Another approach called Canary deployment, is a variation of the blue green deployment. In canary deployments, the green environment is a scaled-down version of the blue environment and is relying on the capability of the router to consistently route a small percentage of the requests to the new green environment, while the bulk of the requests are routed to the blue environment.

Configuration Management

A deployment package that's deployable anywhere shouldn't contain environment specific options or restricted/sensitive data and requires a separate solution. Teams need the ability to manage the configuration and securely get them to the services on startup. Microservice platforms typically have built in solutions that can be leveraged.

Popular approaches for delivering the configuration are:

- **Environment variables**: Load configuration into the environment variables of the service.
- **File system volume**: Mount a file system with the secrets and configuration into the service.
- **Shared key/value store**: Have the service talk to a shared key/value store.

If using environment variables, one thing to watch out for is that they tend to be leaky by default. Exception handlers will grab and ship the environment to a logging platform. Child processes also duplicate the parent's environment on startup. As a result, it is possible to accidentally leak data.

6.4 OPERATIONS

Centralized Logging

Each service instance will generate logs. With a system image as a deployment package, those instances will get replaced every time a new release is deployed. Can't store any logs on those instances, as they would just get lost on the next deployment.

A centralized logging system should be provided to the service teams by the platform. All services should ship their logs to the same logging system in a standardized log format. This approach provides the service teams with the ability to search across all services, within a specific service, or within an instance of a service.

Correlation IDs are used to track the request across multiple other services. When communicating with any service and have the services include them into their log entries. When searched across all services for the correlation ID, should be able to see the timeline of side effects from the original request across all services.

Centralized Monitoring

There is a proliferation of number of deployments because of Microservices architecture. More the moving parts, more the chances of failure, and hence the Monitoring becomes very important for the availability of the overall system. A monitoring mechanism has typically following parts, viz. Measurements (or Metrics), Resolution and Action.

Types of Monitoring

This can be studied from various viewpoints.

Infra level Monitoring

This involves monitoring the storage, CPU consumption, memory consumption and the network characteristics of the hardware the services are deployed on. This will depend on the IAAS or the hosting mechanism. Typically tools like Nagois are used to monitor the infrastructure resources and raise alerts if the service levels are breached. If deployed on IAAS or PAAS platform, respective cloud or Platform management tools will be used. This would be similar between monolith and microservices architectures, just that microservices architecture require this to be done on scale as the number of deployments and hence service infrastructures will be higher.

Monitoring the Software Products or Components

There are other infrastructures such as Messaging, Databases, and HTTP Servers that also need to be monitored for uptime. However, this type of monitoring already exists within an enterprise via a scripting or monitoring tools deployed, and the strategy continues even in Microservices architecture.

Application Services Monitoring

This involves monitoring the application service deployments for uptime, and health. Services can report their health via

- Pull mechanism via JMX, or exposing an HTTP URL where the agents can come and collect the statistics, using Spring actuator
- Push mechanism, the application services can also use Codahale, Spring Actuator or other metrics libraries to send events to Kafka stream or a Graphite installation.

Monitoring Logs

Traditional applications (or monoliths) used to generate one set of logs per deployment, which corresponded to a log containing debug, information and warnings, and another error log, based on logging libraries like Log4j. In Microservices, the problem gets compounded due to the number of microservices calls to fulfil a business process. The information on processing the request can be spread into multiple deployments, and hence tracing the request could get complicated.

Hence, log aggregation may be required to send the logs or the statements to a central location where they can be aggregated, monitored and actions taken accordingly.

Business Level Monitoring

Enterprises can take different strategy for monitoring the business level metrics, often referred to as Business Activity Monitoring (BAM). The individual metrics reported by application services can be aggregated using CEP (Complex Event Processing) to derive business metrics. Alternatively, BAM tools are available in market that track the business processes and requests to build the business metrics.

Monitoring Techniques

By Enterprise tools or products

Traditionally applications were monitored by Enterprise tools such as App Dynamics. Though the same mechanism can be used to monitor the application runtimes, these need to scale better due to the increase in number of instances to be monitored.

Monitoring as a Service

For cloud deployments, using hosted services like "New Relic" is an option, where the enterprise does not have to buy license for a product but subscribes to a service. This could reduce the capital overlay required to get running.

Metrics Aggregation & Analysis

If the Services are using a push model to send their runtime metrics, a sophisticated metrics aggregation and analysis tool can be used to collect metrics and then create various aggregations.

Service Registry and Heart Beats

Typically Dynamic Service Registries like Eureka and Consul also do Service monitoring. Eureka expects Services to report their uptime by sending heartbeats to itself. Consul, on the other hand pings the services regularly to check if they are up and running. In both the approaches, if the services dont respond or send heart beats, the registries refresh their service end point addresses so that the requests will not be directed to the service that has not reported its metrics.

Metrics

The application services can export interesting metrics via the following libraries. This includes uptime, number of times the services were accessed, average response time, memory used, memory free, and other statistics.

1. Spring Actuator - It is a library that can be included by Spring boot applications, which enables to automatically expose the service metrics on various URLs to the end point. For example,
/health & /metrics. The metrics are recorded implicitly.

2. Codahale Metrics - Allows to have a finer control over metrics by recording the metrics explicitly using the metrics API.

These metrics can be continually monitored for change especially degradation. It also gives an indication of which services are frequently used, well behaving and generally more resilient (handle higher load without degradation in response time).

Troubleshooting

Troubleshooting a customer request across microservices could be a challenging task. As discussed earlier, it is important to aggregate the logs to a central location so that searching becomes easier. Another pattern often used in conjunction with this log aggregation pattern is discussed below.

Correlation ids

Every service while handling a request, mandatorily asks for and checks a correlation id (unique id) in the incoming request. If the request contains this id, it is logged with every log statement so that the trail of the logs can be searched using this correlation id. This id is created by the first component that receives the service request and carries to all the downstream service calls. Using Splunk or Elastic Search and Kibana in ELK, it makes it easier to track a service execution using this correlation ids.

Automation

Typically monitoring mechanisms raise alerts when a measured metric exceeds threshold. However, with dev ops and infrastructure as code, it is possible to take corrective actions as part of monitoring actions.

1. **Scale up** - The mechanism which are used to start the service instance first time, can be used to spawn more services when increase in load is detected.

2. **Restart** - If there is a service failure, and the SOP is to restart a service, then the restart can be triggered by a monitoring action.

3. **Scale down** - if the load on the Service dips beyond a certain number of calls, it is possible to call a clean shutdown on the process and delete its endpoint from the service registry.

Auto Scaling

Services that are stateless are easy to scale. Just add more instances as needed behind the load balancer. The information needed to make a scaling decision (CPU/memory usage, etc) can be retrieved from the monitoring platform.

Many microservice platforms have declarative interfaces to handle instance count, which can be quite handy. Tell it how many instances are needed, it makes it happen. All really is needed to implement auto-scaling on such a platform is a way to update the "required instance count" programmatically. As an added bonus, the same process also takes care of failing instances by adding a new one whenever an existing one fails. There is also means like programmable infrastructure. Programmable infrastructure, means writing code using tools like puppet, chef etc. to manage configurations and automate provisioning of infrastructure in addition to deployments.

Backing Services

Services need to talk to external systems. Some examples are: databases, caches, message queues, email delivery systems. These systems can be made available to teams as hosted services provided by a third party or custom services managed within the enterprise. Either way, given the large number of services and environments that may need their own instances of these systems, it's important to have automation around the provisioning and management of these systems.

It's definitely possible to provide a database system with persistent storage and integrate it into the logging and monitoring systems. However, this may not always be practical. Some systems have special infrastructure requirements, especially when considering high availability configurations.

6.5 Ownership

End to End Ownership

Service teams should own, operate and evolve the services they build. Their work is done when the service is retired, not when it is deployed.

With this approach, those who feel the pain of poor architectural decisions are also able to fix them. The additional operational knowledge they gain is valuable input when deciding how to best evolve the service to meet future growth requirements. All of this encourages operational simplicity which ultimately results in improved stability of the services.

Full Stack Teams

When building a number of small services, each team member will be part owner of multiple services. It's important that the team that owns the service has the skills and tools necessary to develop, deploy and operate the service. Team should be fully independent in daily operations so they're able to react quickly to changing business requirements.

People also move around within an organization. Consistency in development, deployment and operations practices across microservices can minimize the learning curve when service ownership changes hands.

Communication gets harder as a team gets bigger. Teams should be big enough that they can get stuff done independently without wasting too much time in the processes that enable them to communicate.

6.6 Developing Microservices

Microservices are typically deployed onto cloud as cloud native application. Deployment of Microservices can be done in multiple ways. Deploying onto PaaS platform like Pivotal Cloud Foundry, deploying onto a virtualized environment (VM) and deploying onto a set of docker containers.

Container are lightweight than virtual machines as they isolate only system resources (like CPU, RAM, disk space) etc on a given operating system. VMs isolate from operating system hence heavy weight and requires a bigger foot print. PaaS platforms provide additional services for development like backing services, infrastructure services like monitoring, load balancing etc.

In order to successfully develop and deploy, below components are required.

- Container tool like Docker, container orchestration/management tool like Docker compose or Kubernetes.
- PaaS platform like cloud foundry, openshift etc.
- Microservices development framework like Spring Cloud, Vert.x etc. These frameworks will either contain or support other required components like service config, discovery, gateway, chassis, monitoring etc.
- Continuous integration infrastructure like Jenkins, Go CD, TeamCity etc.
- Monitoring tools like New Relic, Prometheus etc.
- Security frameworks like oAuth2, OpenID etc.

- Distributed tracing tools like Spring Cloud Sleuth, Zipkin, HTrace etc.

In this chapter we will show how to create Microservices, docker containers and deploy Microservices onto it. We are showing the below code snippets for development purpose, CI will take care of managing the build, container management and deployment once we get into higher environments (like Pre Prod, Prod).

Let's continue our License Management case study from the design (chapter 5) and try to implement. We will use the following frameworks for our development:

1) Docker and Docker Compose.
2) Spring Cloud as the development framework (Spring Framework 5). We will use Git for config server, Eureka for service discovery, Zuul for gateway, Spring Boot for Chassis, Hystrix for resilience (circuit breaker), New Relic for monitoring.
3) Jenkins for continuous integration, Git as source repository
4) oAuth2 as security framework.
5) JDK 1.8

We will divide the development into below categories:

1) Infrastructure components
2) Core services
3) Composite services

Infrastructure components

Following are infrastructure components, setup and configuration of these components will not be detailed in this chapter rather code snippets are shown. Best place to start creating the skeleton code is using http://start.spring.io/ and get the project with all dependencies.

- Creating containers using Docker
- API Gateway
- Authentication
- Service discovery
- Circuit breaker for resilience
- Configuration Server

Below diagram shows the interactions between various components of Microservices architecture.

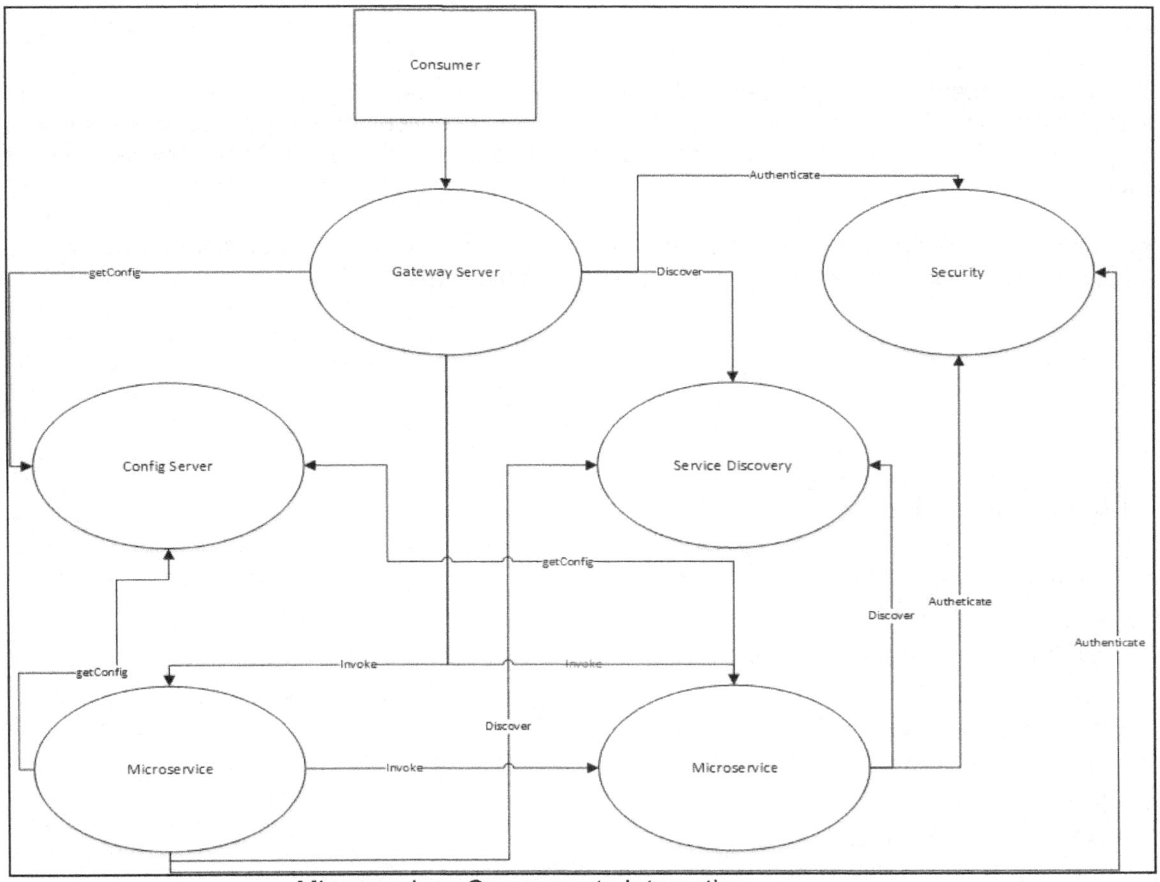

Microservices Components Interaction

Below is the screen shot shows various components selected at start.spring.io to generate a skeleton project.

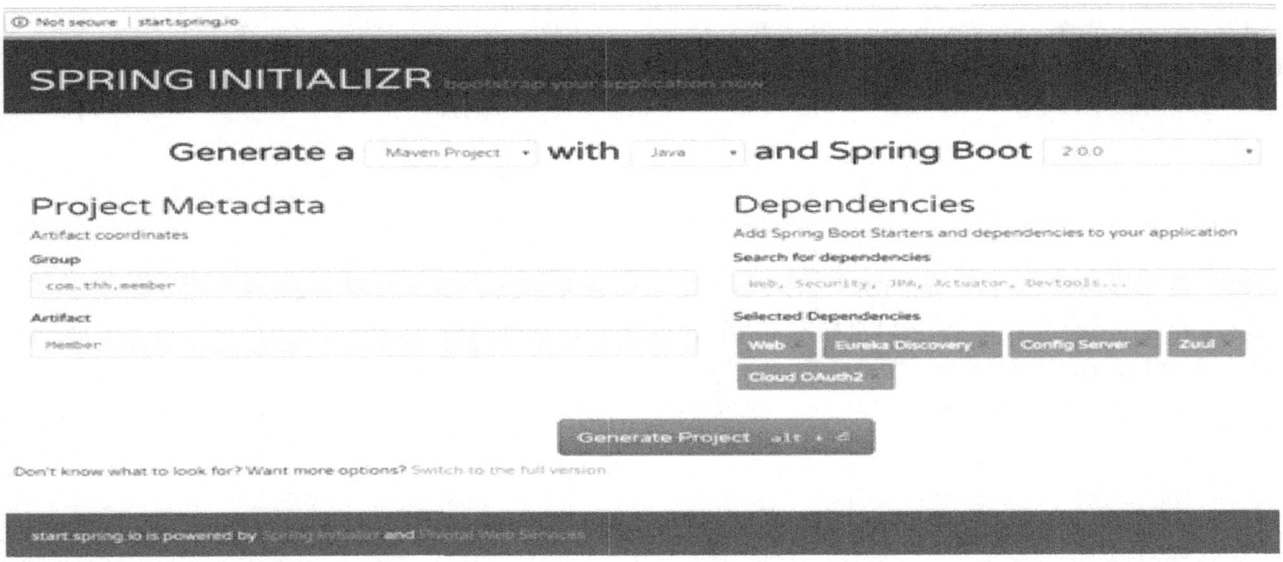

The components required for our development have been selected and can be seen under "Selected Dependencies" section in the above screen shot. We can also create one application for each of the infrastructure components.

Code Snippets:

Config Server

Config server will manage properties (in a properties file) centralized and shared by all Microservices. We will create a config server which is itself a Microservice, and manages all Microservices properties files and those files are versioned controlled; any change in the properties will automatically publish to all Microservices without restarting the services.

Below are the code snippets for spring cloud config server. We are showing only the server part here. Config client will be any application that will use the config server for configurable items.

pom.xml

```
<?xml version="1.0" encoding="UTF-8"?>
<project
xmlns="http://maven.apache.org/POM/4.0.0"
xmlns:xsi="http://www.w3.org/2001/XMLSchema-instance"
xsi:schemaLocation="http://maven.apache.org/POM/4.0.0 http://maven.apache.org/xsd/maven-
4.0.0.xsd">
<modelVersion>4.0.0</modelVersion>
<groupId>com.lms.License/groupId>
<artifactId>ConfigServer</artifactId>
<version>0.0.1-SNAPSHOT</version>
<packaging>jar</packaging>
<name>ConfigServer</name>
<description>BGK Project</description>
<parent>
<groupId>org.springframework.boot</groupId>
<artifactId>spring-boot-starter-parent</artifactId>
<version>2.0.0.RELEASE</version>
<relativePath/>
<!-- lookup parent from repository -->
</parent>
<properties>
<project.build.sourceEncoding>UTF-8</project.build.sourceEncoding>
<project.reporting.outputEncoding>UTF-8</project.reporting.outputEncoding>
<java.version>1.8</java.version>
<spring-cloud.version>Finchley</spring-cloud.version>
</properties>
<dependencies>

<dependency>
<groupId>org.springframework.cloud</groupId>
<artifactId>spring-cloud-config-server</artifactId>
</dependency>
<dependency>
<groupId>org.springframework.boot</groupId>
<artifactId>spring-boot-starter-test</artifactId>
<scope>test</scope>
```

```
</dependency>
</dependencies>
<build>
<plugins>
<plugin>
<groupId>org.springframework.boot</groupId>
<artifactId>spring-boot-maven-plugin</artifactId>
</plugin>
</plugins>
</build>
</Project>
```

Below is the code for config server:

```
package com.lms.license.configserver;

import org.springframework.boot.SpringApplication;
import org.springframework.boot.autoconfigure.SpringBootApplication;
import org.springframework.cloud.config.server.EnableConfigServer;

@EnableConfigServer
@SpringBootApplication
public class ConfigServer {
 public static void main(String[] args) {
  SpringApplication.run(ConfigServer.class, args);
 }
}
```

The Config Server needs to know which repository to manage. There are several choices here, but we'll use a Git-based filesystem repository. Config Server could easily pointed to a Github repository. On the file system, create a new directory and git init it. Then add for example, a file called license.properties (assuming that license is the client application that will use the config server) to the Git repository. Make sure to also git commit it, as well.

Spring application will connect to config Server whose spring.application.name property identifies it as “license” to the Config Server. This is how the Config Server will know which set of configuration to send to a specific client. It will also send all the values from any file named application.properties or application.yml in the Git repository.

Specify the path to the Git repository by specifying the spring.cloud.config.server.git.uri property in config server application.properties as below:

```
server.port=8888
spring.application.name=config
spring.cloud.config.server.git.uri=${HOME}/application-config
```

In the client application (any application that want to use the configuration) application name and the config server URL will be specified in bootstrap.properties as below:

```
spring.cloud.config.name = {application name}
```

```
spring.cloud.config.uri=http://localhost:8888
```
and {application name}.properties in the Git repository. We will show how to add this below.

Service Registry

Service discovery allows services to find and communicate with each other without hard coding hostname and port. Eureka server is responsible to maintain the registry of all the Microservices that have been deployed. Each of the Microservices (called clients) will register themselves and discover other registered microservices. The discovery server expects a regular heartbeat message from each microservice instance. If an instance begins to consistently fail to send a heartbeat, the discovery server will remove the instance from his registry. This way we will have a very stable ecosystem of Microservices collaborating among each other, and address of other Microservice need not be maintained manually. Below is the code snippet for service registry (server part)

pom.xml

```
<?xml version="1.0" encoding="UTF-8"?>
<project
xmlns="http://maven.apache.org/POM/4.0.0"
xmlns:xsi="http://www.w3.org/2001/XMLSchema-instance"
xsi:schemaLocation="http://maven.apache.org/POM/4.0.0 http://maven.apache.org/xsd/maven-4.0.0.xsd">
<modelVersion>4.0.0</modelVersion>
<groupId>com.lms.license/groupId>
<artifactId>EurekaServer</artifactId>
<version>0.0.1-SNAPSHOT</version>
<packaging>jar</packaging>
<name>EurekaServer</name>
<description>Demo project for Spring Boot</description>
<parent>
<groupId>org.springframework.boot</groupId>
<artifactId>spring-boot-starter-parent</artifactId>
<version>1.5.4.RELEASE</version>
<relativePath/>
<!-- lookup parent from repository -->
</parent>
<properties>
<project.build.sourceEncoding>UTF-8</project.build.sourceEncoding>
<project.reporting.outputEncoding>UTF-8</project.reporting.outputEncoding>
<java.version>1.8</java.version>
<spring-cloud.version>Finchley</spring-cloud.version>
</properties>
<dependencies>
<dependency>
<groupId>org.springframework.cloud</groupId>
<artifactId>spring-cloud-starter-eureka-server</artifactId>
</dependency>
</dependencies>
<build>
<plugins>
<plugin>
<groupId>org.springframework.boot</groupId>
<artifactId>spring-boot-maven-plugin</artifactId>
</plugin>
</plugins>
</build>
</Project>
```

Below is the code for service registry:

```
package com.lms.license.registryserver;
```

```
import org.springframework.boot.SpringApplication;
import org.springframework.boot.autoconfigure.SpringBootApplication;
import org.springframework.cloud.netflix.eureka.server.EnableEurekaServer;
@EnableEurekaServer
@SpringBootApplication
public class EurekaServerApplication {
 public static void main(String[] args) {
  SpringApplication.run(EurekaServerApplication.class, args);
 }
}
```

Gateway

Zuul is the front door for all requests from devices and web sites to the backend applications. As an edge service application, Zuul is built to enable dynamic routing, monitoring, resiliency and security. Multiple API gateways' can be there for each kind of client this pattern is called Backend for frontend.

Below diagram depicts the pattern:

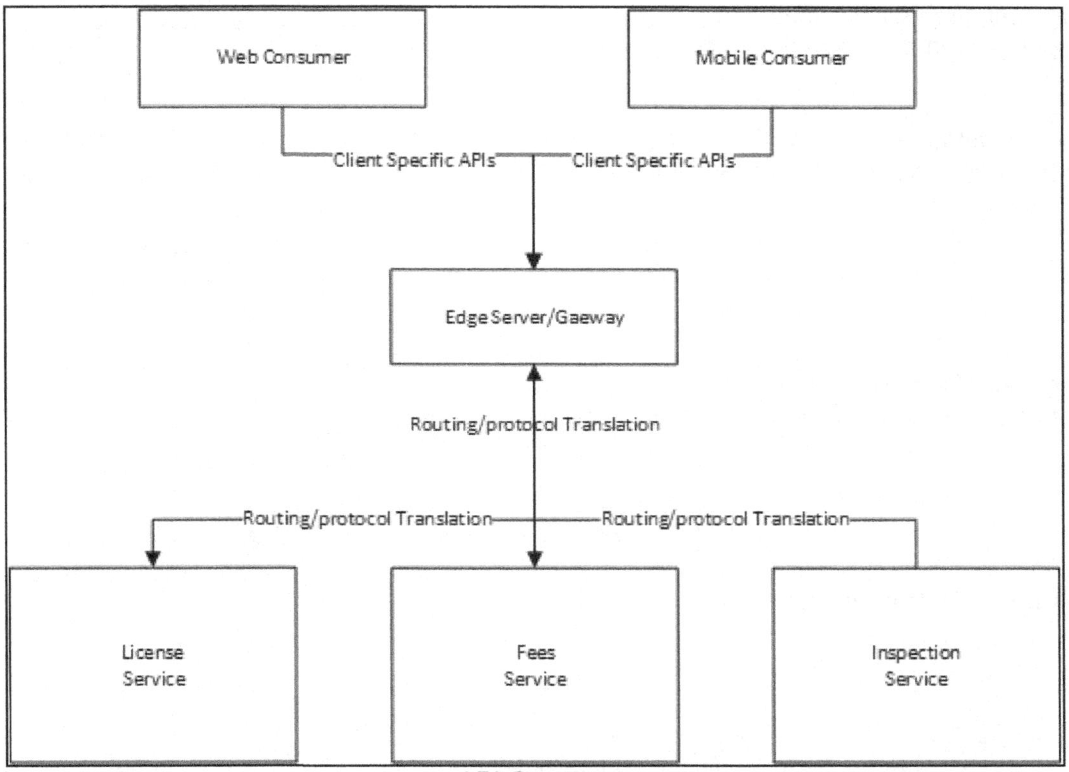

API Gateway

pom.xml:

```
<?xml version="1.0" encoding="UTF-8"?>
<project
xmlns="http://maven.apache.org/POM/4.0.0"
xmlns:xsi="http://www.w3.org/2001/XMLSchema-instance"
xsi:schemaLocation="http://maven.apache.org/POM/4.0.0 http://maven.apache.org/xsd/maven-4.0.0.xsd">
<modelVersion>4.0.0</modelVersion>
<groupId>com.lms.license/groupId>
<artifactId>EdgeServer</artifactId>
<version>0.0.1-SNAPSHOT</version>
<packaging>jar</packaging>
```

```
<name>EdgeServer</name>
<description>Demo project for Spring Boot</description>
<parent>
<groupId>org.springframework.boot</groupId>
<artifactId>spring-boot-starter-parent</artifactId>
<version>1.5.4.RELEASE</version>
<relativePath/>
<!-- lookup parent from repository -->
</parent>
<properties>
<project.build.sourceEncoding>UTF-8</project.build.sourceEncoding>
<project.reporting.outputEncoding>UTF-8</project.reporting.outputEncoding>
<java.version>1.8</java.version>
<spring-cloud.version>Finchley</spring-cloud.version>
</properties>
<dependencies>
<dependency>
<dependency>
<groupId>org.springframework.cloud</groupId>
<artifactId>spring-cloud-starter-zuul</artifactId>
</dependency>
<dependency>
<groupId>org.springframework.boot</groupId>
<artifactId>spring-boot-starter-test</artifactId>
<scope>test</scope>
</dependency>
</dependencies>
<build>
<plugins>
<plugin>
<groupId>org.springframework.boot</groupId>
<artifactId>spring-boot-maven-plugin</artifactId>
</plugin>
</plugins>
</build>
</Project>
```

Zuul service proxy / Edge Service

```
package com.lms.license.gateway;

import org.springframework.boot.SpringApplication;
import org.springframework.boot.autoconfigure.SpringBootApplication;
import org.springframework.cloud.netflix.zuul.EnableZuulProxy;

@EnableZuulProxy
@SpringBootApplication
public class GatewayApplication {

  public static void main(String[] args) {
    SpringApplication.run(GatewayApplication.class, args);
  }
}
<project.reporting.outputEncoding>UTF-8</project.reporting.outputEncoding>
<java.version>1.8</java.version>
<spring-cloud.version>Finchley</spring-cloud.version>
</properties>
<dependencies>
```

```
<dependency>
<dependency>
<groupId>org.springframework.boot</groupId>
<artifactId> spring-boot-starter-web</artifactId>
</dependency>
<dependency>
<groupId>org.springframework.boot</groupId>
<artifactId>spring-boot-starter-test</artifactId>
<scope>test</scope>
</dependency>
</dependencies>
<build>
<plugins>
<plugin>
<groupId>org.springframework.boot</groupId>
<artifactId>spring-boot-maven-plugin</artifactId>
</plugin>
</plugins>
</build>
</Project>
```

```
package com.lms.license

import org.springframework.boot.SpringApplication;
import org.springframework.boot.autoconfigure.SpringBootApplication;
import org.springframework.web.bind.annotation.RequestMapping;
import org.springframework.web.bind.annotation.RestController;
import com.lms.data.LicensePre;
```

```
@RestController
@SpringBootApplication
public class LMSLicense{

  @RequestMapping(value = "/license/licenses", method=RequestMethod.POST)
  public String ApplyForLicense(@RequestBody LicensePre licensePre) {
  String url = "http://localhost/license/licenses";
  LicensePre lPre = restTemplate.postForObject(url, licensePre, LicensePre.class);

   return lPre.getStatus();
  }

  public static void main(String[] args) {
    SpringApplication.run(LMSLicense.class, args);
  }
}
```

bootstrap.properties in src/main/resources

bootstrap.properties

```
spring.cloud.config.name=lmslicense
spring.cloud.config.discovery.service-id=config
spring.cloud.config.discovery.enabled=true
eureka.client.serviceUrl.defaultZone=http://localhost:8761
```

lmslicense.properties (Add this file to Git repository)

```
spring.application.name=license
server.port=8090
eureka.client.region = default
eureka.client.registryFetchIntervalSeconds = 5
```

Hystrix

Hystrix is the fault tolerance library. We'll implement the Circuit Breaker enterprise pattern, which is describing a strategy against failure cascading at different levels in an application.

The principle is analogous to electronics: Hystrix is watching methods for failing calls to related services. If there is such a failure, it will open the circuit and forward the call to a fallback method.

The library will tolerate failures up to a threshold. Beyond that, it leaves the circuit open. Which means, it will forward all subsequent calls to the fallback method, to prevent future failures. This creates a time buffer for the related service to recover from its failing state.

pom.xml:

```
<?xml version="1.0" encoding="UTF-8"?>
<project
xmlns="http://maven.apache.org/POM/4.0.0"
xmlns:xsi="http://www.w3.org/2001/XMLSchema-instance"
xsi:schemaLocation="http://maven.apache.org/POM/4.0.0 http://maven.apache.org/xsd/maven-4.0.0.xsd">
<modelVersion>4.0.0</modelVersion>
<groupId>com.lms.license</groupId>
<artifactId>CircuitBreaker</artifactId>
<version>0.0.1-SNAPSHOT</version>
<packaging>jar</packaging>
<name>CircuitBreaker </name>
<description>Demo project for Spring Boot</description>
<parent>
<groupId>org.springframework.boot</groupId>
<artifactId>spring-boot-starter-parent</artifactId>
<version>1.5.4.RELEASE</version>
<relativePath/>
<!-- lookup parent from repository -->
</parent>
<properties>
<project.build.sourceEncoding>UTF-8</project.build.sourceEncoding>
<project.reporting.outputEncoding>UTF-8</project.reporting.outputEncoding>
<java.version>1.8</java.version>
<spring-cloud.version>Finchley</spring-cloud.version>
</properties>
<dependencies>
<dependency>
<dependency>
<groupId>org.springframework.cloud</groupId>
<artifactId> spring-cloud-starter-netflix-hystrix</artifactId>
</dependency>
<dependency>
<groupId>org.springframework.boot</groupId>
<artifactId>spring-boot-starter-test</artifactId>
```

```
<scope>test</scope>
</dependency>
</dependencies>
<build>
<plugins>
<plugin>
<groupId>org.springframework.boot</groupId>
<artifactId>spring-boot-maven-plugin</artifactId>
</plugin>
</plugins>
</build>
</Project>
```

Below is the class with hystrix command and fallback option.

```
package com.lms.license;

import com.netflix.hystrix.contrib.javanica.annotation.HystrixCommand;
import org.springframework.stereotype.Service;
import org.springframework.web.client.RestTemplate;

import java.net.URI;

@Service
public class LicenseService {

  private final RestTemplate restTemplate;

  public LicenseService (RestTemplate rest) {
    this.restTemplate = rest;
  }

  @HystrixCommand(fallbackMethod = "licensefallback")
  public List<License> getlicenses) {
    URI uri = URI.create("http://localhost:8080/license-service"); // Notice that we are not invoking the license-se//rv
ice directly. We are going thru the gateway server

    return this.restTemplate.getForObject(uri, LicensePre.class);
  }

  public String licensefallback () {
    return "licensefallbackmessage";
  }

}
```

If call to getLicense fails then the circuit is open and fallback method will be called till the original method recovers. The original method getLicense and fall back method licensefallback should be in the same class.

Authentication

Below code shows how to configure oAuth2 using spring application. Scenario is how to configure spring application with a social application (like facebook or twitter) for single sign on. Below diagram shows the flow between various components involved in authentication in a web application.

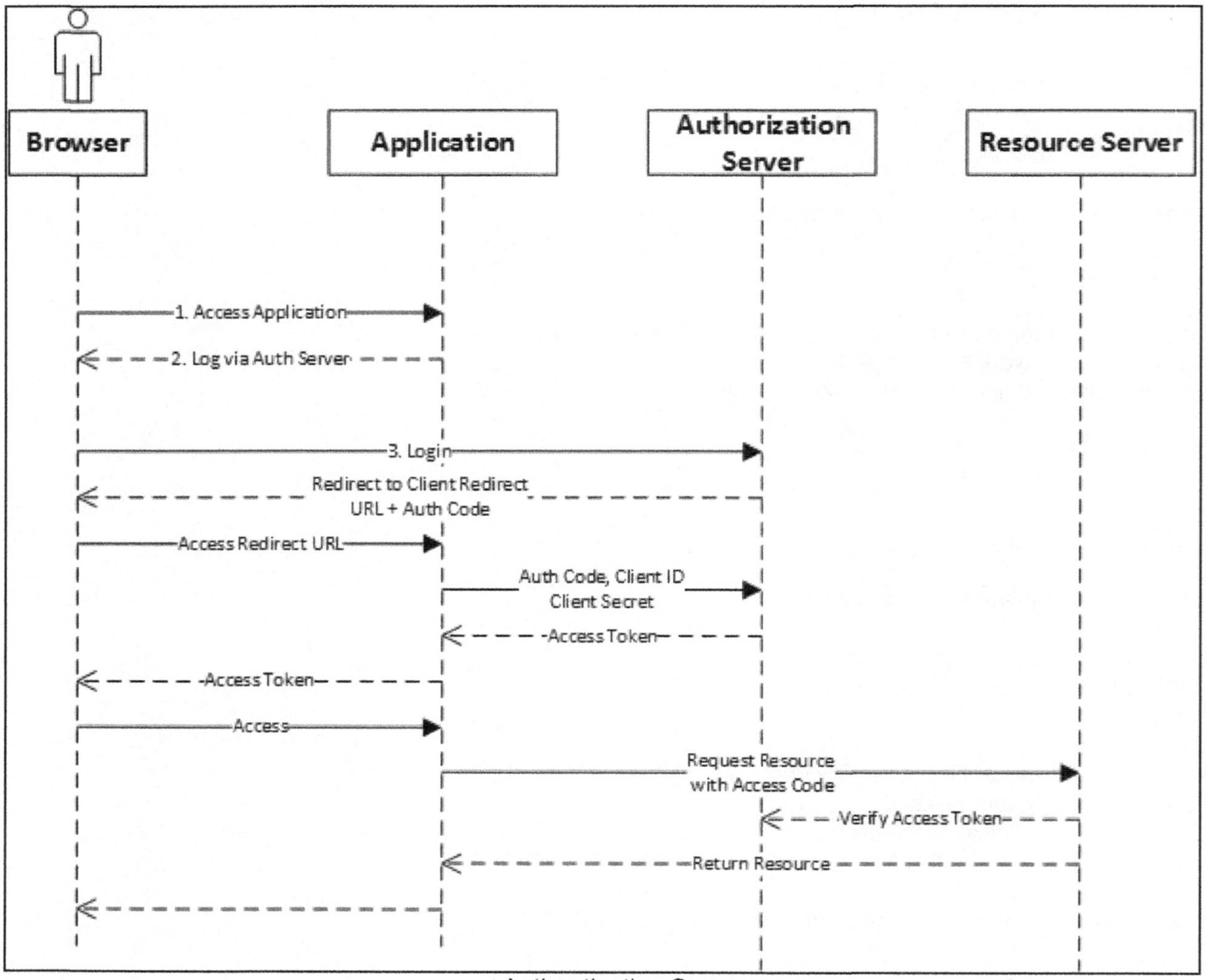

Authentication Sequence

`pom.xml:`

```
<?xml version="1.0" encoding="UTF-8"?>
<project
xmlns="http://maven.apache.org/POM/4.0.0"
xmlns:xsi="http://www.w3.org/2001/XMLSchema-instance"
xsi:schemaLocation="http://maven.apache.org/POM/4.0.0 http://maven.apache.org/xsd/maven-4.0.0.xsd">
<modelVersion>4.0.0</modelVersion>
<groupId>com.lms.license</groupId>
<artifactId>security</artifactId>
...

<dependency>
            <groupId>org.springframework.boot</groupId>
            <artifactId>spring-boot-starter-security</artifactId>
</dependency>
<dependency>
```

```
        <groupId>org.springframework.security.oauth</groupId>
        <artifactId>spring-security-oauth2</artifactId>
</dependency>
...
```

To enable social application (ex: Facebook):

SocialApplication.java

```
@SpringBootApplication
@EnableOAuth2Sso
public class SocialApplication {
...
}
```

Configuration

application.yml

```
security:
  oauth2:
    client:
      clientId: 233668646673605
      clientSecret: 33b17e044ee6a4fa383f46ec6e28ea1d
      accessTokenUri: https://graph.facebook.com/oauth/access_token
      userAuthorizationUri: https://www.facebook.com/dialog/oauth
      tokenName: oauth_token
      authenticationScheme: query
      clientAuthenticationScheme: form
      resource:
        userInfoUri: https://graph.facebook.com/me
...
```

The process is to register our application with the external social application (Facebook in this case) and get the details like clientID, clientSecret and redirect URL (like a home page for our application) post registration. User will be redirected to the login page of the external social application once he tries to open the home page. If authentication is successful user will be redirected to the redirect URL with an access token. More details can be obtained by looking into appropriate oAuth2 resources.

Now let's realize the case study design done in chapter 5. Below are the core and aggregate/composite services that are mapped to each of the task in the license issue business process

Core services

All the entity and value objects identified during the design will be implemented as core services. Below is the list of core services along with their bounded context.

Sno	Core Service Name	Bounded Context	Task (from Business Process)
1	LicenseService	License	Apply For License
2	LicenseProcessingService	License	Associate Multiple Licenses
3	LicenseService	License	View List of Licenses
4	LicenseIssuanceService	License	Approve License
5	InspectionService	Inspection	Create Inspection Requisition
6	InspectionService	Inspection	Record Information about Inspection
7	FeesService	Fees	Pay the fees

Below is the code snippets for License and inspection core services:

LicenseService

```
package com.lms.license;

import java.util.ArrayList;

import org.springframework.beans.factory.annotation.Autowired;
import org.springframework.jdbc.core.JdbcTemplate;
import org.springframework.stereotype.Controller;
import org.springframework.web.bind.annotation.RequestMapping;
import org.springframework.web.bind.annotation.RequestMethod;
import org.springframework.web.bind.annotation.ResponseBody;

import com.fasterxml.jackson.core.JsonProcessingException;
import com.fasterxml.jackson.databind.ObjectMapper;
import com.lms.data.License;
import com.lms.data.LicenseRowMapper;

@Controller
public class LicenseService{

		@Autowired
		JdbcTemplate jdbcTemplate;

		// getLicenses method to return all licenses. This returns JSON as output

		@ResponseBody
		@RequestMapping(value="/getLicenses", method = RequestMethod.GET, produces = "application/json
")
   public String getLicenses() {
		//String jsonInString = null;
		ArrayList<License> flist =null;
		StringBuffer sBuffer = new StringBuffer();
		String query="SELECT * from License";
		try {
				ObjectMapper mapper = new ObjectMapper();

				// Connect to the DB and retrieve the data
		 flist =	(ArrayList<License>) jdbcTemplate.query(query,new LicenseRowMapper(),null);
				System.out.println("list size is:"+flist.size());

				flist.forEach((license) -> {
						try {
								sBuffer.append(mapper.writeValueAsString(license));
						} catch (JsonProcessingException e) {
								e.printStackTrace();
						}
				});
		}catch (Exception e) {
				e.printStackTrace();
		}
		 return sBuffer.toString();
   }
}
```

We need to add two properties files:

bootstrap.properties in src/main/resources:

```
spring.cloud.config.name=license-service
spring.cloud.config.discovery.service-id=config
spring.cloud.config.discovery.enabled=true
eureka.client.serviceUrl.defaultZone=http://localhost:8761
```

license-service.properties (Add this file to Git repository)

```
spring.application.name=license-service
server.port=8083
eureka.client.region = default
eureka.client.registryFetchIntervalSeconds = 5
eureka.client.serviceUrl.defaultZone=http://localhost:8761
```

InspectionService

```
package com.lms.inspection;

import java.util.ArrayList;

import org.springframework.beans.factory.annotation.Autowired;
import org.springframework.jdbc.core.JdbcTemplate;
import org.springframework.stereotype.Controller;
import org.springframework.web.bind.annotation.RequestMapping;
import org.springframework.web.bind.annotation.RequestMethod;
import org.springframework.web.bind.annotation.ResponseBody;

import com.fasterxml.jackson.core.JsonProcessingException;
import com.fasterxml.jackson.databind.ObjectMapper;
import com.lms.data.Inspection;
import com.lms.data.InspectionRowMapper;

@Controller
public class InspectionService{

	@Autowired
	JdbcTemplate jdbcTemplate;

	// getInspectionDetails method gets details of an inspection. This returns
JSON as output

		@ResponseBody
		@RequestMapping(value="/inspection/inspections/{inspectionID}", method
= RequestMethod.GET, produces = "application/json")
	    public String getInspectionDetails( @PathVariable("inspectionID") String
inspectionID ) {
		//String jsonInString = null;
		ArrayList<Inspection> flist =null;
		StringBuffer sBuffer = new StringBuffer();
		String query="SELECT * from Inspections where INSPECTION_ID=
"+inspectionID;
		try {
			ObjectMapper mapper = new ObjectMapper();
```

```
                // Connect to the DB and retrieve the data
            flist =     (ArrayList<Inspection>) jdbcTemplate.query(query,new
InspectionRowMapper(),null);
                System.out.println("list size is:"+flist.size());

                flist.forEach((inpsection) -> {
                    try {

        sBuffer.append(mapper.writeValueAsString(inpsection));
                    } catch (JsonProcessingException e) {
                        e.printStackTrace();
                    }
                });
            }catch (Exception e) {
                e.printStackTrace();
            }
            return sBuffer.toString();
        }
}
}
```

We need to add two properties files:

bootstrap.properties in src/main/resources:

```
spring.cloud.config.name=inspection-service
spring.cloud.config.discovery.service-id=config
spring.cloud.config.discovery.enabled=true
eureka.client.serviceUrl.defaultZone=http://localhost:8761
```

inspection-service.properties (Add this file to Git repository)

```
spring.application.name=inspection-service
server.port=8084
eureka.client.region = default
eureka.client.registryFetchIntervalSeconds = 5
eureka.client.serviceUrl.defaultZone=http://localhost:8761
```

Aggregate/Composite services

All the aggregates and other services identified during design will be implemented as aggregate/composite services. Below is the list of composite services.

Sno	Composite Service Name	Bounded Context	Task (from Business Process)
1	LicenseServiceAggregate	License	New License
2	InspectionAggregate	Inspection	Inspection Required (Yes)
3	ReportAggrgate	Reports	Record Information about Inspection

Below is the code snippet for LicenseServiceAggregate

```
package com.lms.license;

import org.springframework.beans.factory.annotation.Autowired;
import org.springframework.jdbc.core.JdbcTemplate;
import org.springframework.web.bind.annotation.RequestBody;
```

```
import org.springframework.web.bind.annotation.RequestMapping;
import org.springframework.web.bind.annotation.RequestMethod;
import org.springframework.web.bind.annotation.ResponseBody;
import org.springframework.web.client.RestTemplate;

import com.lms.data.Inspection;
import com.lms.data.License;
import com.lms.data.LicensePre;

public class LicenseServiceAggregate {

      @Autowired
      JdbcTemplate jdbcTemplate;

      // getInspections method to return all inspections. This returns JSON as
output

      @ResponseBody
      @RequestMapping(value="/license/licenses", method = RequestMethod.POST)
    public LicensePre ApplyForLicense(@RequestBody LicensePre licensePre) {

            RestTemplate restTemplate = new RestTemplate();

      // Check with CGLS system,fees payment has been omitted in the code.
      // We will start with inspection for issuing license

      //Create new inspection to record the inspection findings

      // We are invoking the gateway rather than accessing inspection and license
      service directly

      String iurl = "http://localhost:8080/inspection-service/inspections";
      Inspection inspection = licensePre.getInspection();
    restTemplate.postForObject(iurl,inspection, Inspection.class);

    // View license details to record inspection findings
    String lurl = "http://localhost:8080/license-
service/licenses{"+licensePre.getLicense().getLicenseID()+"}";
    License license = restTemplate.getForObject(lurl, License.class);

    //Issue license (update license status and intimate the applicant)

    LicensePre lpre = new LicensePre();
    lpre.setStatus("Success");
    return lpre;
}
}
```

We need to add two properties files:

bootstrap.properties in src/main/resources:

```
spring.cloud.config.name=licenseaggregate-service
spring.cloud.config.discovery.service-id=config
spring.cloud.config.discovery.enabled=true
eureka.client.serviceUrl.defaultZone=http://localhost:8761
```

licenseaggregate-service.properties (Add this file to Git repository)

```
spring.application.name= licenseaggregate-service
```

```
server.port=8085
eureka.client.region = default
eureka.client.registryFetchIntervalSeconds = 5
eureka.client.serviceUrl.defaultZone=http://localhost:8761
```

6.7 Summary

Proper implementation of Microservices makes the enterprise agile to changes in business and boost time to market. The cost and time to develop and deliver applications will greatly decrease, and systems will become more resilient. Microservices bring a change in enterprise communication that enriches development and operations teams to formulate, strategize, and deliver in more efficient ways.

Tools, patterns, processes and people play a crucial role in implementing Microservices properly. These help the team to develop and manage Microservices effectively and efficiently. Tools cut across design, development, deployment, tracing and monitoring. As number of Microservices grow, automation using tools will be necessary to manange them. New processes like Continous Integration and Delivery, Decenatralized Governance needs to be put in place to enable frequent releases using Microservices platform.

7. Microservices and DevOps

7.1 Introduction to DevOps

In traditional development, the development team and operations team always work in silos and the team raise the fingers against each other. Development team focus on functionality, features, user experience, architecture, maintainability. The focus of operations team is always cost, reliability, security, risk and manageability.

To bring these two teams on common platform and make them work as a single team is a big challenge.
The idea is to de-silo Development and Operations to overcome the bottlenecks in the software development and deployment process, mostly on the ops side. The goal of DevOps is to support a continuous delivery pipeline.

DevOps is the set of concepts, cultural philosophies, practices, team organization structures and tools that increases an organization's ability to deliver applications and services at high velocity to the clients. Organizations that adopt DevOps are more easily able to release and monitor Microservices. It helps in responding to new requirements quickly, or to problems that occur in production. This speed enables organizations to better serve their customers and compete more effectively in the market.

DevOps aims to decrease the time between applying a change to a system and the change being transferred to the production environment, but also insists on keeping the software quality in terms of both code and the delivery mechanism as one of the key elements in the development process. Any techniques that enables the mentioned goal is considered as a DevOps practice.
The objective of DevOps is, Maximize the predictability, efficiency, security and maintainability of operational processes. This objective is supported by automation. DevOps targets product delivery, quality testing, feature development and maintenance releases in order to improve reliability and security and faster development and deployment cycles.
DevOps promotes the, agile methods to operations. It provides the collaboration between development and operations teams.

DevOps commonly includes the following processes,

- Agile practices, brining Agile methods to operations
- Continuous integration
- Release automation
- Functional unit testing
- System integration testing
- Service and infrastructure monitoring

7.2 How DevOps Works

By adopting DevOps model, development and operations teams are no longer "siloed." Sometimes, these two teams are merged into a single team where the engineers work across the entire application lifecycle, from development and test to deployment to operations, and develop a range of skills not limited to a single function.
DevOps Team use practices to automate processes that are traditionally manual and slow. The team use a technology stack and tooling which help to operate and evolve applications quickly and reliably. These tools also help engineers independently accomplish tasks.

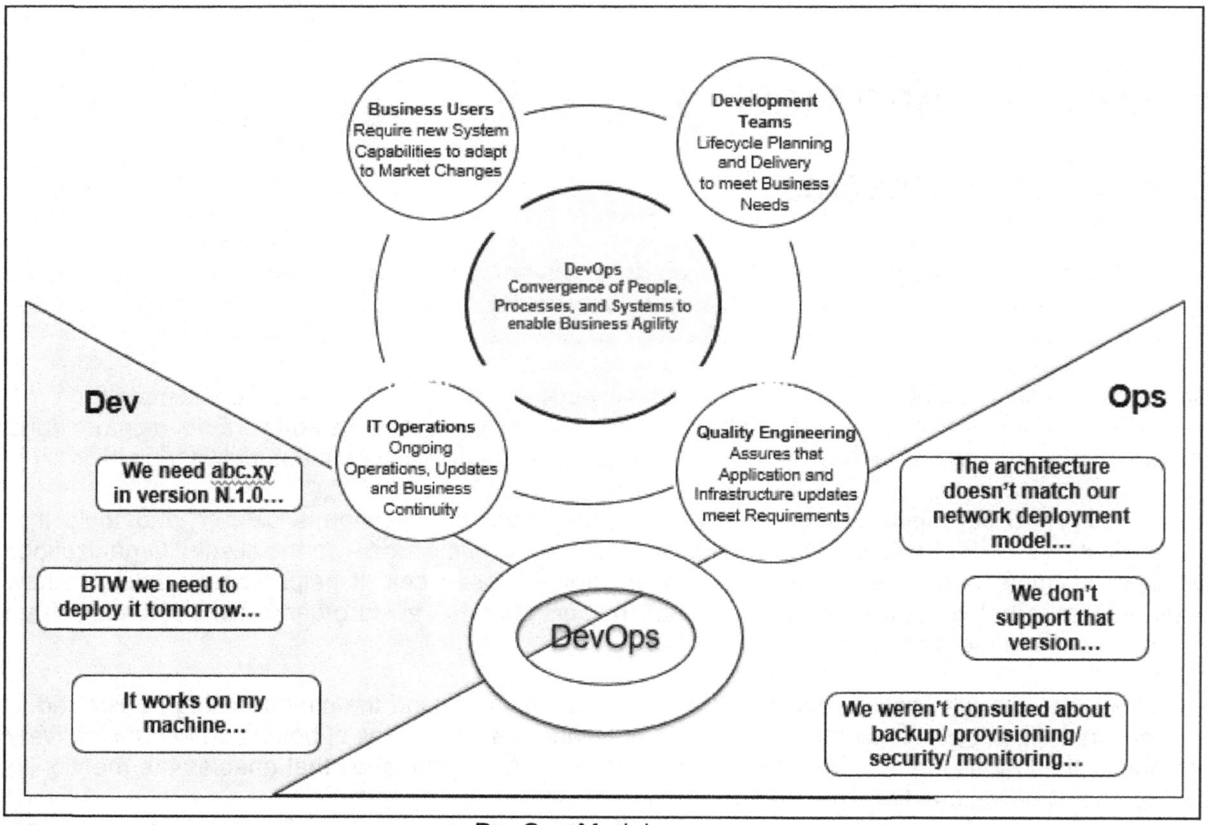

DevOps Model

For example, deploying code or provisioning infrastructure, normally require help from other teams, and this further increases the team's velocity.
The following are the outcome of the DevOps adoption,

- Faster Time to market
- Increases the customer satisfaction
- Better employee productivity and happiness
- Lower failure rate of new releases
- Faster time to recovery
- Improved deployment frequency
- Shortened lead time between fixes
- Maximize the predictability, efficiency, security and maintainability of operational processes.

Although DevOps practices can also be used for monoliths, but Microservices enables an effective implementation of the DevOps through promoting the importance of small teams.

7.3 DevOps Capabilities for Microservices

The Common challenges that affect a traditional software delivery are listed below,

1. Everything needs software
2 Software runs on a server to become a service
3. Delivering a service from inception to its users is too slow and error-prone
4. There are internal friction points that make this the case.
5. Defects released into production.
6. inability to diagnose production issues quickly
7. Problems appear in some environments only; Blame shifting or finger pointing
9. Long delays while dev, QA, ops team waits on resource/response from other teams.
10. Releases slip or fail - Delay causes money loses.
11. Traditional Thinking:

- Dev's job is to add new features; Ops' job is to keep the site stable and fast.

As monolithic applications are incrementally functionally decomposed into foundational platform services and vertical services, we no longer just have a single release team to build, deploy, and test the application. Microservices architecture results in more frequent and greater numbers of smaller applications being deployed. DevOps enables to do more frequent deployments, and to scale to handle the growing number of new teams releasing Microservices.

DevOps achieves continuous delivery, which is required for a Microservices architecture, through its three pillars approach,

- Automation
- Standardization
- Frequent code releases
- Culture

Automation: As depicted in Figure below, every traditional *hand off* point is automated in a DevOps approach. Automation begins from provisioning of the infrastructure and configuration of the platform for the workloads. This is followed by the automation of application deployment, database changes, and other application-related configurations.

Finally, maximum benefits in a DevOps approach are gained through test automation in the form of unit tests, system integration tests, and user acceptance tests. Because Microservices represent small, composable business functions, the level of automation possible through a DevOps approach aligns perfectly for its development lifecycle.

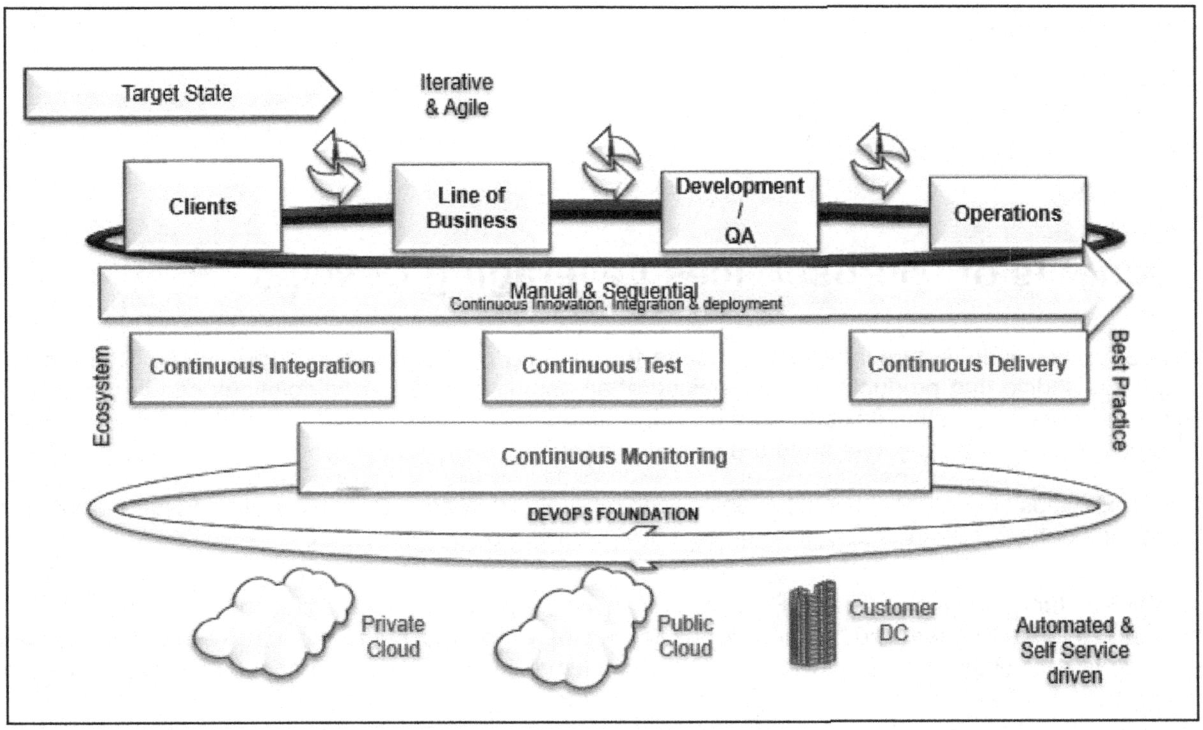

DevOps approach to software development: Continuous delivery

Standardization: In DevOps model the standardization can easily be confused with the flexibility that a Microservices architecture provides with regards to technology and data store stack. In a DevOps world, standardization is to reduce risk by adopting the following factors.

- Using standard platforms
- Reliable and repeatable process
- High level of confidence by the time the artefact is ready to release

Frequent Releases: This keeps the applications relevant to business needs and priorities. Smaller releases mean lesser code changes, and that helps reduce risk significantly.

With smaller release cycles, it is also easier to detect bugs much earlier in the development lifecycle. Quick feedback from the user base also supports code adaptability. All of these characteristics of a DevOps approach augur well for Microservices development.

Culture: Transitioning to DevOps requires a change in culture and mind set. At its simplest, DevOps is about removing the barriers between two traditionally siloed teams, development and operations. In some organizations, there may not even be separate development and operations teams; engineers may do both. With DevOps, the two teams work together to optimize both the productivity of developers and the reliability of operations. They strive to communicate frequently, increase efficiencies, and improve the quality of services they provide to customers. They take full ownership for their services, often beyond where their stated roles or titles have traditionally been scoped by thinking about the end customer's needs and how they can contribute to solving those needs. Organizations using a DevOps model, regardless of their organizational structure, have teams that view the entire development and infrastructure lifecycle as part of their responsibilities.

7.4 Principles of DevOps

Principles of DevOps are,

- Iterative
- Incremental
- Continuous
- Automated
- Collaborative
- Holistic

7.5 Benefits of Microservices Leveraging DevOps

Microservices based architecture introduces change for creating next generation applications. Those embracing that change are finding that productivity is increasing at an astonishing rate, and solutions can be delivered much more quickly to those requesting flexible, scalable applications.
In the field of DevOps, Microservices bring the following benefits,

Speed: The DevOps model enables developers and operations teams to achieve the faster adoption of the business to the changing markets and grow more efficient driving business results.

Rapid Delivery: Innovation and Faster Production can be achieved by increasing the frequency and pace of releases. The quicker we can release new features and fix bugs, the faster we can respond to Organization customer needs and build competitive advantage. Continuous integration and continuous delivery are practices that automate the software release process, from build to deploy.
Deployability: Microservices offer increased agility, which fuels the ability to roll out new versions of a service. That agility is due to shorter build, test, and deploy cycles.
Availability: Releasing a new version of a particular Microservice requires very little downtime, whereas rolling out a new version of a service in the monolithic application normally requires a full restart of the entire monolith.

Scalability: Microservices can be scaled independently using pools, clusters, grids. That deployment characteristic makes Microservices a great match for the elasticity of the cloud. Operate and manage infrastructure and development processes at scale. Automation and consistency help to manage complex or changing systems efficiently and with reduced risk. For example, infrastructure as code helps to manage development, testing, and production environments in a repeatable and more efficient manner

Modifiability: DevOps provides the flexibility to consume new frameworks, libraries, data sources, and other resources. As loosely coupled, modular components, Microservices prove to be easier to work with and support dynamic discovery and binding via a registry

Management: Microservices can leverage the agile methodology, where the application development effort is divided across teams that are smaller and work more independently.

Improved Collaboration: Build more effective teams under a DevOps cultural model, which emphasizes values such as ownership and accountability. Developers and operations teams collaborate closely, share many responsibilities, and combine their workflows. This reduces inefficiencies and saves time.
For example, Reduced handover periods between developers and operations, writing code that takes into account the environment in which it is run.
Security: DevOps use automated compliance policies, fine-grained controls, and configuration management techniques for security management. For example, using infrastructure as code and policy as code, we can define and track compliance at scale
Microservices bring additional productivity to DevOps by embracing a common toolset, which can be used for both development and operations. That common toolset establishes common terminology, as well as processes for requirements, dependencies, and problems.
This makes easier for Devs and Ops to work with one another, allowing those entities to work jointly on a problem, and successfully fix a build configuration or build script. DevOps and Microservices work better when applied together.

7.6 DevOps Framework Adoption

The combination of Microservices and increased release frequency leads to significantly more deployments which can present operational challenges. DevOps practices covering Continuous Integration and Continuous Delivery solve these issues and the organizations deliver rapidly in a safe and reliable way.

Together, these practices help organizations deliver faster, more reliable updates to their customers. Here is an overview of important DevOps practices. DevOps framework addresses continuous delivery through a series of continuous steps,

- Continuous Planning
- Continuous Development
- Continuous Deployment
- Continuous Testing
- Continuous Monitoring
- Continuous Feedback

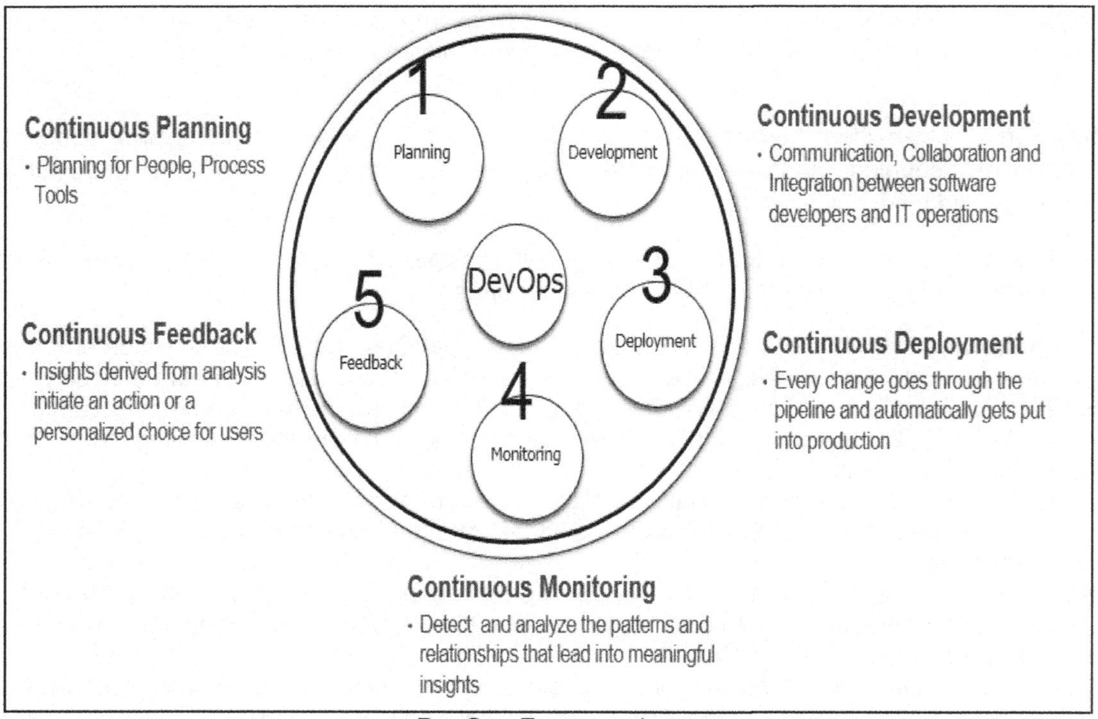

DevOps Framework

Generally, DevOps Services provide the following capabilities,

- Agile planning, through the Track & Plan service
- A web integrated development environment (IDE) for editing and managing source control
- Source control management (SCM) through Git, Jazz SCM, or GitHub
- Automated builds and deployments, through the Delivery Pipeline service

The following sections describe these DevOps capabilities, and explain how they are useful in context of Microservices.

Continuous business planning

Continuous business planning, helps to continuously plan, measure, and bring business strategy and customer feedback into the development lifecycle. It provides the tools and practices to help organizations *do the correct things* and focus on activities where they can gain most value,

- Attacking the high-value and high-risk items first
- Predicting and quantifying the outcomes and resources
- Measuring honestly with distributions of outcomes
- Learning what customers really want
- Steering with agility

Continuous business planning employs lean principles to start small by identifying the outcomes and resources needed to test the business vision and value, to adapt and adjust continually, measure actual progress, learn what customers really want, shift direction with agility, and update the plan. A plan to deploy DevOps that involves people, process and tools has to be in place.

- Define a target
- Establish a transformation plan
- Manage plan execution

Continuous business planning has the following benefits,

- Helps continuously plan business needs and prioritize them
- Integrate customer feedback with business strategy
- Align customer feedback into the development lifecycle as business needs

- Focus on *doing the correct things*
- Prioritize business needs that adds the most value

Continuous development

DevOps emphasizes communication, collaboration and integration between business, software developers, Quality Assurance (QA) and IT operations to deliver innovative, quality software continuously. DevOps recognizes the interdependence of software development and IT operations and helps an organization produce software and IT services more rapidly, with frequent iterations. This includes support for polyglot programming, multi-platform development, elaboration of ideas, and creation of user stories, complete with cross-team change and lifecycle management. DevOps is predicated on the idea that all elements of technology infrastructure can be controlled through code. With the rise of the cloud it can all be done in real-time via a web service.

Collaborative development includes the practice of continuous integration, which promotes frequent team integrations and automatic builds. By integrating the system more frequently, integration issues are identified earlier, when they are easier to fix.

Collaborative development has the following benefits,

- Bringing together customer and IBM team stakeholders toward a partnered goal
- Focused on delivering a tangible and functional business outcome
- Working within a time-boxed scope
- Using common tools and process platform (customer, traditional, or IBM Cloud)

Continuous integration

Enhanced integrations and capabilities to synchronize software testing with deployment and operations. Continuous Integration (CI) is a development practice that requires developers to integrate code into a shared repository several times a day. Each check-in is then verified by an automated build, allowing teams to detect problems early. By integrating regularly, we can detect errors quickly, and locate them more easily.
Integrations are verified by an automated build that runs regression tests to detect integration errors as quickly as possible. Teams find that this approach leads to significantly fewer integration problems, and enables development of cohesive software more rapidly. By integrating the system more frequently, integration issues are identified earlier, when they are easier to fix.

The overall integration effort is reduced using continuous feedback, and the project shows constant and demonstrable progress. Continuous integration has the following benefits,

- Each developer integrates daily, leading to multiple integrations per day.
- Integrations are verified by automated builds that run regression tests to detect integration errors as quickly as possible.
- Small, incremental, frequent builds help with early error detection, and require less rework.
- Continuous integration is a leading practice to make a global collaborative development work successfully.

Configuration Management

Configuration management solves the problem of having to manually install and configure packages once the hardware is in place. The benefit of using configuration automation solutions is that servers are deployed exactly the same way every time. Any change across thousands of servers, we need to make the change at one place.

Continuous release and deployment

Continuous Deployment is wherein every change goes through the pipeline and automatically gets put into production, resulting in many production deployments every day with greater delivery speed and frequency for complex applications. It reduces the amount of manual labor, resource wait-time, and rework by using push-button deployments that enable a higher frequency of releases, reduced errors, and end-to-end transparency for compliance.

Continuous Delivery is the extension of Continuous Integration, achieved by continuously integrating the software by the development team, building executables and running automated tests on the executables to detect problems. Executables are released into production like environments to ensure software works in Production Because every change is delivered to a staging environment using complete automation, the application can be deployed to production with one click when the business is ready. Continuous release and deployment provides a continuous delivery pipeline that automates deployments to test and production environments.

Continuous deployment has the following benefits,

- The leading practice of deploying code rapidly and safely into production-like environments is followed.
- Deployments start automated tests to ensure that components perform business functions as expected.
- Every change is automatically deployed to staging.
- Deployments are on-demand and self-service.
- Applications can be deployed into production with the push of a button, when business is ready.

Configuration Management

Configuration management solves the problem of having to manually install and configure packages once the hardware is in place. The benefit of using configuration automation solutions is that servers are deployed exactly the same way every time. If you need to make a change across ten thousand servers, only need to make the change in one place.

Continuous testing

Continuous Testing strategy promotes the organization wide cultural change to achieve capabilities like test early, test faster, test often and automate. Continuous testing reduces the cost of testing while helping development teams balance quality and speed. It eliminates testing bottlenecks through virtualized dependent services, and simplifies the creation of virtualized test environments that can be easily deployed, shared, and updated as systems change. These capabilities reduce the cost of provisioning and maintaining test environments, and shorten test cycle times by enabling integration testing earlier in the lifecycle.
Continuous testing,

- Synchronizes Testing/QA with Dev and Ops processes optimized to achieve business and development goals
- Encourages a systematic approach toward process improvement.
- Brings real-time assessments, objective go/no-go quality gates and continuous measurements to refine the development process so that business expectations are continuously met

Testers hold all their test artifacts (requirements, epics/user stories, test cases and scenarios, test data, execution lists and results) and their interdependent links in a multi-project, multi-user repository.
The following list describes some of the benefits of continuous testing,

- Avoidance of unexpected disruption to business
- More reliable applications
- Proactive problem prevention
- More effective and quicker testing
- Less rework
- More efficient and happier workers
- Lower operational costs and improved top line

Continuous monitoring

Monitoring and alerting are crucial to manage operations and to ensure people are notified when infrastructure and related services go down. Continuous monitoring across all phases of the application development, testing and deployment is crucial for a successful Agile DevOps implementation.
Continuous monitoring offers enterprise-class, easy-to-use reporting that helps developers and testers understand the performance and availability of their application, even before it is deployed into production. The early feedback provided by continuous monitoring is vital to lowering the cost of errors and change, and for steering projects toward successful completion.

Capabilities to improve service quality by monitoring application performance and Log management solves the problem of aggregating, storing, and analysing all logs in one place.

The operations team manages and ensures that the application is performing as wanted, and that the environment is stable using continuous monitoring. The Operation team need to ensure that the applications are performing at optimal levels, down to levels lower than system monitoring tools would allow. The Operation team works with Dev to build self-monitoring or analytics gathering capabilities directly into the applications being built. This would allow for true end-to-end monitoring, continuously.

Continuous monitoring has the following benefits,

- The leading practice of managing the infrastructure, platform, and applications to ensure that they are functioning optimally is followed
- Thresholds can be set for what is considered optimal.
- Any untoward incident triggers an automatic alert or remediation.
- Monitoring logs are used for operational analytics.
- Developers can also self-monitor applications and look at real-time reports.

Continuous Feedback

Continuous customer feedback and optimization provides visual evidence and full context to analyse customer behaviour and understand customer experiences using web or mobile applications. DevOps showing how instrumented feedback, included with sponsor users connected into cross functional feature teams able to act quickly, can be an incredible combination.

Continuous customer feedback and optimization provides the following benefits,

- Provide clients the ability to gain insight with intuitive reporting and optimized web, mobile, and social channels
- Empower stakeholders, including end-users
- Provide and assess important feedback, from idea through live-use
- Respond with insight and rapid updates
- Maintain and grow competitive advantage

7.7 Summary

The success of DevOps in an enterprise can be achieved by,

- High-trust cultural norms
- Architecture that lends itself to testability and deployability
- Cluster of technical practices that includes continuous integration, continuous delivery, automated deployment, and proactive production monitoring

DevOps is a prerequisite to being able to successfully adopt Microservices at scale in an organization. Teams that have not yet adopted DevOps must invest significantly in defining release processes and corresponding automation and tools. Need to on board new service teams that helps in achieving efficient release and testing of Microservices.

Also, each Microservice team must create their own DevOps infrastructure and services, which results in higher development costs. It also means inconsistent levels of quality, security, and availability of Microservices across teams.

One of the most common business drivers for adopting Microservices is business agility. Microservices allow us to respond quickly and incrementally to business opportunities. Incremental and more frequent delivery of new capabilities drives the need for organizations to adopt DevOps practices.

8. Microservices Governance

8.1 Introduction

Governance is a method or approach to establish policies, standards and best practice guidelines on the adoption of Microservices to enable enterprise agile IT environment.

The governance framework defines a detailed architecture and design approach to be used as a reference to build flexible enterprise services and processes.

In the Microservices world, the developers have a freedom to experiment with new languages, patterns, frameworks, data stores, and other innovative aspects of IT development. On the other hand, Operations team can be very uncomfortable when confronted with that level of experimentation from the development. There are some concerns about Microservices architecture being without any governance, or having a thin governance compared to service-oriented architecture (SOA).

The Microservices governance framework is established with the emphasis on the following:

Business

- Strategic alignment of IT with Business: Derive IT vision, goals and objectives and align it efforts in line with the Business vision
- Reusability of services and quick-time-to production

Technical

- Microservices Reference Architecture: Base line architecture guideline for service design and integration with enterprise usage systems etc
- Identifying, specifying, creating, and then deploying Microservices Services through DevOps methodology
- Enterprise wide service policies, common infrastructural services
- Developing fine-grained services by composition and orchestration
- Service monitoring and management: Management and monitoring of access policies, Quality of Service (QoS) metrics and KPIs to gauge performance and throughput

Organizational

- Establishing a dedicated enterprise to govern effective management
- Enterprise structure as to who should make critical decisions
- How will these decisions be made and monitored

The following diagram depicts the overview of the Microservices Governance covering 3 key aspects of the governance, people, technology and processes.

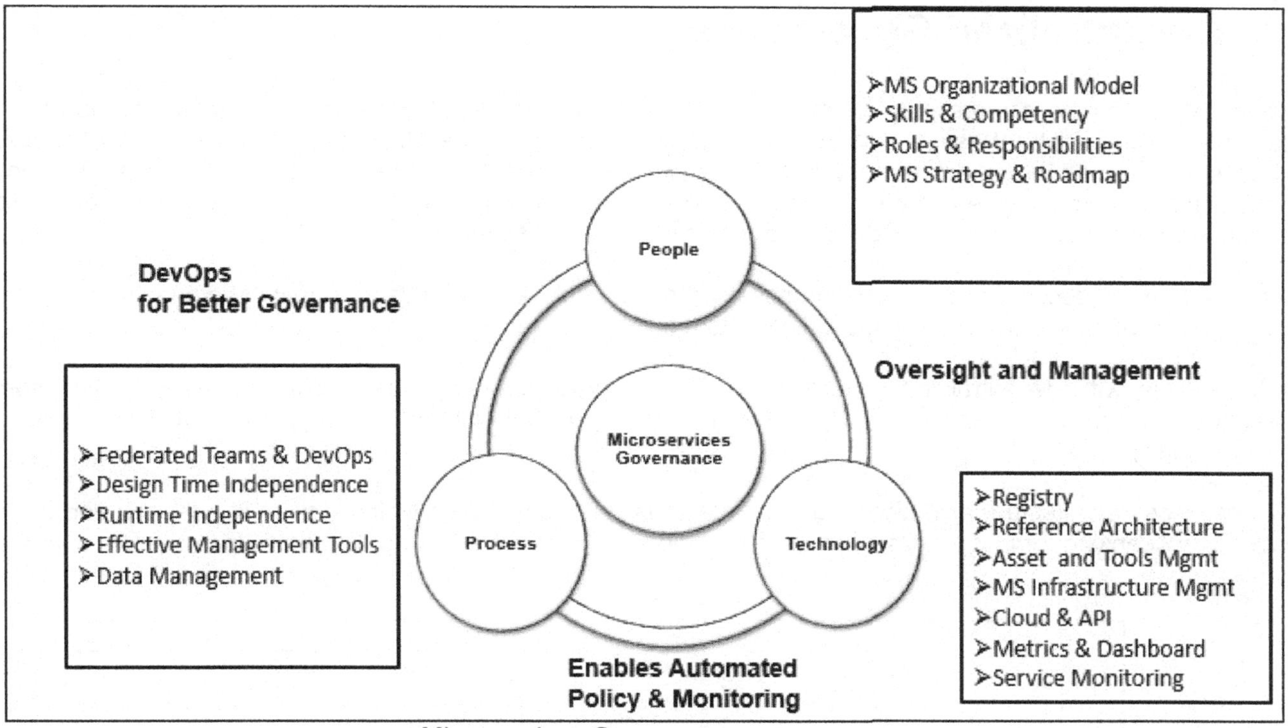

Microservices Governance

8.2 Importance of Microservices Governance

Governance with monoliths are centralized. Decisions are made top-down, rigid control is maintained to ensure standards are in place across the organization and within the application stack. Over time, this model degenerates, creating a stagnant technological and architectural system, thus minimizing innovation.

The failure to implement proper governance mechanism can result in a brittle and unmanageable architecture where a distributed mess of services that offer poor business support will flourish unchecked.

Microservices governance facilitates a higher return from all enterprise investments and business benefits by establishing policies, lucid communication channels, and ones where effectiveness and accountability can be measured and quantified.

Guiding Principles

Prior to establishing the foundational elements, every organization needs to define the guiding principles and follow them.

Here are some key guiding principles for establishing successful Microservices governance,

- **Independent Services**: A Microservice is independent of all other services. Independence of services enables rapid service development & deployment. Requires both design & runtime independence of services
- **Single Responsibility:** Focuses on one. Requires business function, decomposition into granular
- **Self-Containment:** A Microservice is self-contained, independent deployable unit. In order for a Microservice to be independent, it needs to include all necessary building blocks for its operation, contained within.
- **Policies & Best practice guidelines**: Compliance to Microservices Domain Reference Architectures, Governance Processes and Roadmap

8.3 Decentralized Governance

Microservices promote a more polyglot model regarding technology stack for supported languages, tools, and data stores. Reusability of assets and tools are the core concept of the Microservices, rather than centralized forceful standards. Other salient features of Microservices are functional isolation, localized scalability, and ease of maintenance. All of features come as part of being a self-contained, fully consumable, fine-grained application with decentralized governance that satisfies a specific micro business function.

Central theme of decentralization governance is the concept of build it and run it. Microservices team is responsible for all aspects of the service delivery from build to run to fix.

The key value with decentralized governance is that a proof point can be quickly established, with some knowledge of return on investment (ROI) and a time frame for that, without incurring extensive risks regarding time and money.

A Microservices architecture also decentralizes data store decisions. Whether the reason is best of breed for the workload, or licensing, or just a skills decision, the choice of a data store technology is left up to the Microservices team.

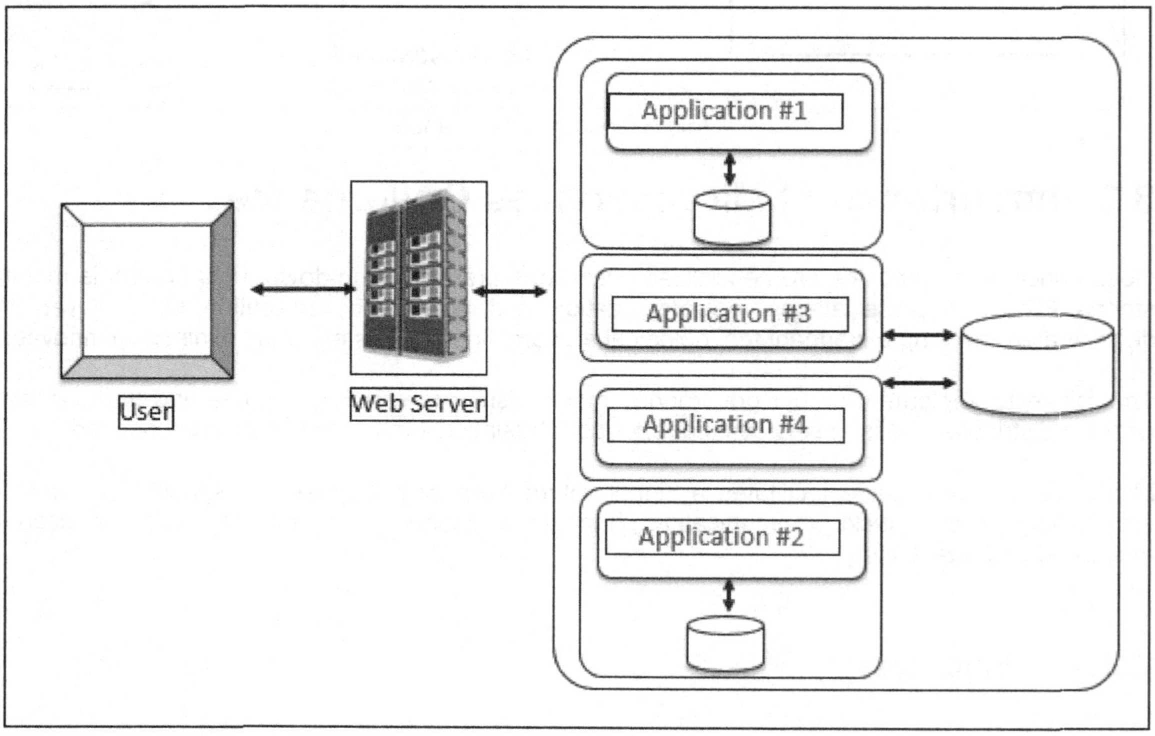

Decentralized data store for Microservices

Decentralized governance gives teams the freedom to develop software components using different stacks. For example, an engineering organization should not try to decree all the specifics of how software is built by each team but it should define some global standards that apply to the methodology behind the software. A couple examples of good standards are:

- All code should be run through a bug analysis before merge
- All teams should use a peer code review process

In Microservices environment, developers add and remove functionalities all the time. They change the code, replace core elements of the application, and so on, all the time implying that Microservices are constantly evolving. API's are leveraged to establish the interaction between the Microservices, which helps the application to work properly. Also, the version control mechanism establishes the services interface between old and new services.

The benefits of that Microservices provide can be reaped with careful planning, innovative design thinking, and the proper operational and managerial structure.

Other aspects to be considered about centralized versus decentralized governance are monitoring, logging, single sign-on, backups, operational metrics, and reporting.

However, the following services need to follow the centralized governance. Common services across domains, and the scope and size of each Microservice.

- Central logging service, logging is centrally available for any analytics and reporting
- Sign-on service, it is integrated to some form of an enterprise-wide directory service
- Monitoring and backup service, Information about monitored units, the frequency of monitors and alerts
- Reporting about any issues and their workloads, are all determined and managed centrally
- Backup frequency, testing the cadence of restore scripts, and data retention procedures

8.4 People

The Microservices architecture team is focused primarily on managing and monitoring the enterprise activities. Which includes designing the enterprise application based on Microservices technology. The team provides the right function to end users and the appropriate operational support for the new architecture.

Microservices Organizational Model

In enterprise-level Microservices adoption, the team structure and skills play a major role rather than the underlying technology. Flat organization structures, flexible teams, and cross-functional abilities are crucial to the success of Microservice adoption.

Forming a capable, skilled team requires realigning staff around functionality rather than architecture.

Establishing a DevOps practice before transitioning to Microservices is the best approach which helps in determining communication strategies in advance.

Skilled Teams

In enterprise level Microservices adoption, the team structure and skills play a major role rather than the technology. Flat organization structure and flexible team and cross functional abilities are the key for the success of the Microservices adoption.

Achieving an effective, skilled team requires realigning staff around functionality rather than architecture

Establishing a DevOps practice before transitioning to Microservices is the best approach which helps in determining communication strategies in advance.

The focus of Microservices architecture team is managing and monitoring the enterprise activities in designing the application to provide the right function to end users and have the appropriate operational support for the new architecture.

Microservices team consists of various members with different skill sets such as system analysts, UX/UI designers, backend and frontend developers, etc. The teams are responsible for their project (Microservice) from end to end – from development and deployment to operations, monitoring, and management.

The size of the teams will be determined by the overall size of the enterprise and the project that they are developing. Our experience says that, the ideal size is 8-10 people per team.

In Microservices architecture, the growth of the business will scale the Microservices team. Every team will have a collaborative platform to complete objectives for the project. This ensures deadlines are met, leading to a more efficient and effective product launch.

Microservices Strategy & Roadmap

DevOps Strategy: Reducing the development to deployment cycle time is crucial. Rather than deploying one application, the team will deploy multiple services.

Agile Environment: Services are developed by teams in increments; short phases allow the team to release frequently. This strategically positions the businesses progress. CI/CD should be followed, to increase the level of resilience.

Data Strategy: A robust Master Data Management strategy is required to support the distribution of the data. Consumption of Core data of an enterprise, done by multiple Microservices which are stored in their local databases

8.5 Technology

Reference Architecture

Microservices is not a product, framework, or platform. It is a strategy for building large enterprise distributed systems. Microservices architecture benefits enterprises in multiple ways. Advantages include independent scalability of diverse application components to faster, easier software development and maintenance. Sizing of the Microservices is critical for the design of quality services. Microservices reduce vendor lock-in and eliminate long-term technology commitment. Overall, helping decision makers choose the tools needed to meet IT and business goals.

Microservices Reference Architecture:

- Provides ready-to-use blueprints for building Microservices based systems, speeding – and improving – development.
- Create a platform for testing new features, whether developed internally or externally.
- Helps understand partner systems and components to enterprises to gain a holistic perspective on the Microservices ecosystem.

Registry

As the enterprise grows, tracking the number of Microservices can be a challenge due to their continuous deployment. To solve this challenge, the usage of dynamic registries will help by tracking the deployed services. These registries provide consumers lookup addresses to easily monitor services.

Tools

When building a high scalable architecture using Microservices, tools are required to manage additional services and application components, which include:

- Service discovery tools, e.g., Kubernetes.

- Packaging standards for containerizing applications, g., Docker, and orchestration tools for replicating containers at scale, e.g., Kubernetes. OpenShift by Red Hat includes both of these proven open source technologies.

- CI environment creation tools, g., Jenkins or Shippable for Docker and Kubernetes. Dependency resolution tools, e.g., Nexus.

- Failover and resiliency tools, including libraries such as Hystrix and Ribbon.

Service monitoring, alert, and event tools, e.g., ELK (ElasticSearch, LogStash, and Kibana) stack.

Cloud & API

API is used to establish the interaction between the Microservices, which helps the application to work properly. In addition, the version control mechanism establishes the services interface between new and old services.

Infrastructure Management

Infrastructure management monitors storage, CPU consumption, memory consumption, and hardware network characteristics for deployed services. Infrastructure resources are monitored by Nagois, which raises alerts whenever service levels are breached. If a service is deployed on an IAAS or PAAS platform then the respective cloud or platform management tools are used.

Service Monitoring

Service monitoring happens when the application service deploys for uptime and monitors the health. Services can report their health by Pull mechanism via JMX, or exposing an HTTP URL where the agents can collect the statistics, using Spring Actuator Push mechanism.

8.6 Process

Federated Teams & DevOps

In Microservices environments developers continuously add and remove functionalities. These changes can consist of a change to the code or replacing core elements of the application. While these changes take place, Microservices constantly evolve. An application is broken down to multiple interdependent services. Large, siloed teams are broken into small, multifunctional teams. Which coincides with the progression from development, testing and IT that are transforming into smaller DevOps teams. It is efficient to have the team who built the Microservice own its implementation and maintenance. This benefits the current functioning and future evolution of the service.

Design Time Independence

Defining and controlling the service creations, design, and implementation of service policies.

Runtime Independence

SLAs, throttling, monitoring, common security requirements and service discovery are not covered at each Microservice level. API Gateway helps to realize Runtime governance at a dedicated component level.

Data Management

Unlike SOA, Microservices do not share data. Each Microservice has a separate physical data store and polyglot persistence which allows a variety of database engines to run under each Microservice.

However, maintaining multiple copies of an enterprise database can increase licensing costs and complexity.

Generic extract, transform, and load (ETL) or data virtualization tools can help with data normalization, event sourcing is a well-known design pattern that helps align data stores to adjust to retroactive changes.

8.7 Enterprise Transformation for Microservices

Adoption of Microservices is the evolution of the enterprise transformation. Enterprise transformation is the aggregation of Architecture transformation, process transformation through DevOps, organization transformation and Monitoring. All these together leads to better ROI for an enterprise.

As part of Architectural transformation, identification and decomposition of business functions into Independently manageable units or workloads is done.

In process transformation, automation of environment provisioning to automation of deployments and releases, all play a key part in reducing manual resource demands, number of errors, and a truly agile way to deliver software.

An organizational transformation is essential for the process transformation to succeed. With DevOps, new job roles are created, and existing ones are redefined. Skills training and a new way of thinking become crucial for success. With large enterprises, this means that there might be new partnerships with vendors and service providers to supplement skills.

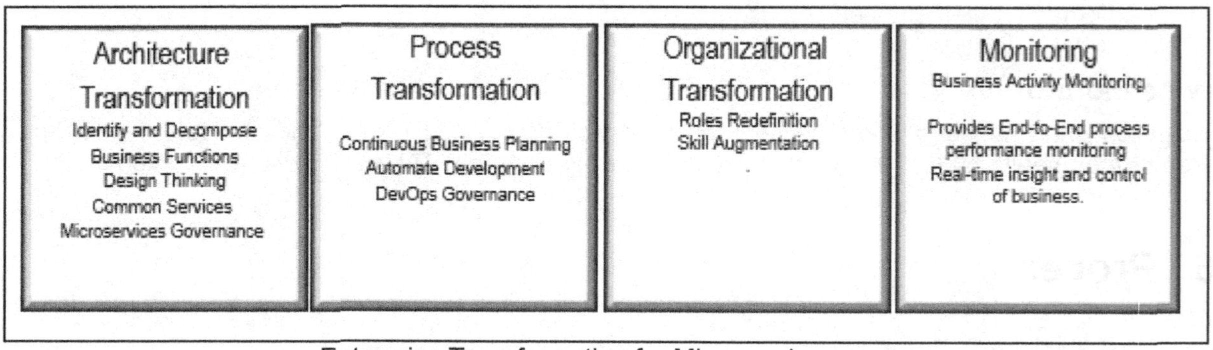

Enterprise Transformation for Microservices

The concept of build it, run it is often talked about with Microservices. There is always resistance to change with large enterprises, so executive commitment and coaching becomes critical during transformation.

8.8 Summary

In summary, Microservices adopt decentralized governance, these standards enable the team to efficiently build and deploy the code that have been created according to individual governance plans. The goal of decentralized governance is to free dev teams, allowing them to allocate time to solving development problems effectively within a timely manner. It is important to develop a DevOps mindset within the enterprise. This mindset empowers developers to control how their governed components are built and operated.

9. Microservices Maturity Model

9.1 Introduction

A Maturity Model is a structured collection of parameters that describe certain aspects of Maturity in an enterprise.

As the Microservices Architecture matures, predictability, process controls and effectiveness also increase. Development of the Enterprise wide Microservices Architecture is critical because it provides the rules and definition necessary for the integration of information and services at the operation level across the Enterprise boundaries.

There exist many different architecture definition approaches for implementing Microservices across Industry. A 71% of companies will intensify their usage of Microservices in 2017 [1]. Many of them are unique and specific to the needs of individual development teams. Many enterprises, without understanding, have been using an approach towards leveraging APIs that classified as Microservices.

Many organizations know that they need to improve their Business and IT alignment in order to successfully manage change, but do not know how. Such organizations typically either spend very little on process improvement, because they are unsure how best to proceed; or spend a lot, on a number of parallel and unfocused efforts, to little or no avail. Many organizations continue to use old monoliths and only create new components as Microservices. The main reason companies have slowdown in adopting Microservices is because of missing knowledge and lack of qualified people [2-3].

An evaluation of the Enterprise practices against the model — called an "assessment" — determines the level at which the organization currently stands. It indicates the organization's maturity in the area concerned, and the practices on which the organization needs to focus in order to see the greatest improvement and the highest return on investment. As the Microservices Architecture Matures the predictability, process controls and effectiveness increases.

Microservices Architecture progresses in Maturity will benefit enterprise the following:

- ❖ Focus on Business Need
- ❖ Agility, enterprises can introduce new products or enhancements into the market quickly
- ❖ Enhancing the customer experience
- ❖ Can be developed & deployed independently of other services
- ❖ Reduced dependency on key resources
- ❖ Improved accuracy in scheduling software development / implementation
- ❖ More efficient deployment of technology solutions
- ❖ Increased traceability

The Microservices adoption challenges by an Enterprise are listed below,

Feature	Challenges
Deployment Complexity	• More Deployment Units • Runtime Monitoring and Maintenance
Duplication	• Reference and Master Data • Domain Layer Code
Testing	• Larger Estate to test • End to End Testing

Coupling	• Existing Services often have coupling at Database Level
More Failure Points	• As number of runtime units increase, so does probability of failure
Tech Proliferation	• More Choices of Implementation
Lack of Maturity	• Few Successful Enterprise Adoptions outside start ups

Based on authors interactions with various enterprise clients, the following are the high level queries raised by them,

- What would it take to become a Matured Microservices enterprise
- What is the roadmap for the enterprise
- What is the Microservices Maturity Model and where do they stand
- What are the architectural foundation pre-requisites for the Microservices adoption
- What are the infrastructural pre-requisites for the Microservices

Many enterprises, without understanding have been using various strategies like, "leveraging APIs that classified as Microservices", "Domain driven design", "SOA the right Way" and "adoption of DevOps Architecture". This demands a need for designing Microservices that adopted across the Enterprises.

All the above had prompted the authors to create a Microservices Maturity model, which helps the enterprise customers to know where they stand and what it would take them to do in order to become a matured Microservices based enterprise. In addition, this Maturity Model is to provide guidance to teams that are already using Microservices on what could be the next improvement.

This Chapter describes the steps towards assessing the Maturity of an Enterprise in a Microservices Architecture Stream covering the aspects of the Enterprise adoption of domain driven design, infrastructure for provisioning and adoption of DevOps.

9.2 Maturity Assessment

Microservices adoption needs some careful thoughts. A quick Maturity assessment will be helpful to understand the Maturity of the enterprise in Microservices adoption and some of the challenges the enterprise can expect.

The main drivers for the Enterprise Microservices Architecture adoption are,

- Enterprise primary business revolves around extremely high volume transactions
- Rapid development and enhanced operational support, reduce implementation and release cycle time and enables continuous delivery
- Enterprises migrating from Monolithic and Legacy Processes to Microservices
- Scalability and flexibility of Cloud service help in handling more customers simultaneously without interrupting service
- For the solutions that require the integration of business capability from disparate systems and programming models
- For aligning business and IT functionality
- For business and technology agility
- Better ROI

- For incremental development (Agile) and continuous deployment of business software

In addition, development of the Enterprise wide Microservices adoption is an ongoing process and cannot delivered overnight. The establishment of a Microservices across Enterprise is critical because it provides the rules and definition necessary for the integration of information and services at the operation level across enterprise boundaries.

9.3 Microservices Maturity Assessment Framework

A Microservices Maturity Assessment framework comprises a maturity model with different maturity levels, a set of parameters that assessed methodology and a toolkit for assessment (questionnaires, tools, etc.). The outcome is a detailed assessment report, which describes the maturity of the enterprise as a whole, as well as the maturity against each of the Maturity assessment parameters.

The key components of this framework depicted below:

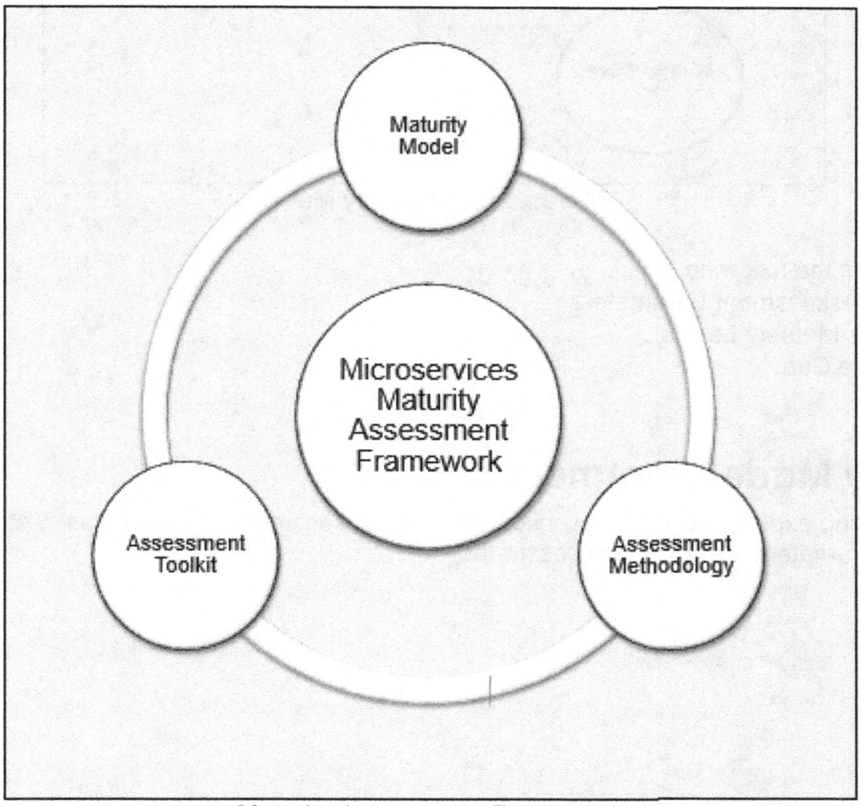

Maturity Assessment Framework

Microservices Maturity Model (MSMM) helps to conduct the Maturity assessment across Enterprise. MSMM provides the framework that represents the key components of a productive enterprise architecture process. The goal is to enhance the overall success of enterprise Microservices adoption by identifying weak areas or examining the existing areas and suggesting changes/improvements to be fit for Microservices, providing a defined evolutionary path to improving the overall adoption process.

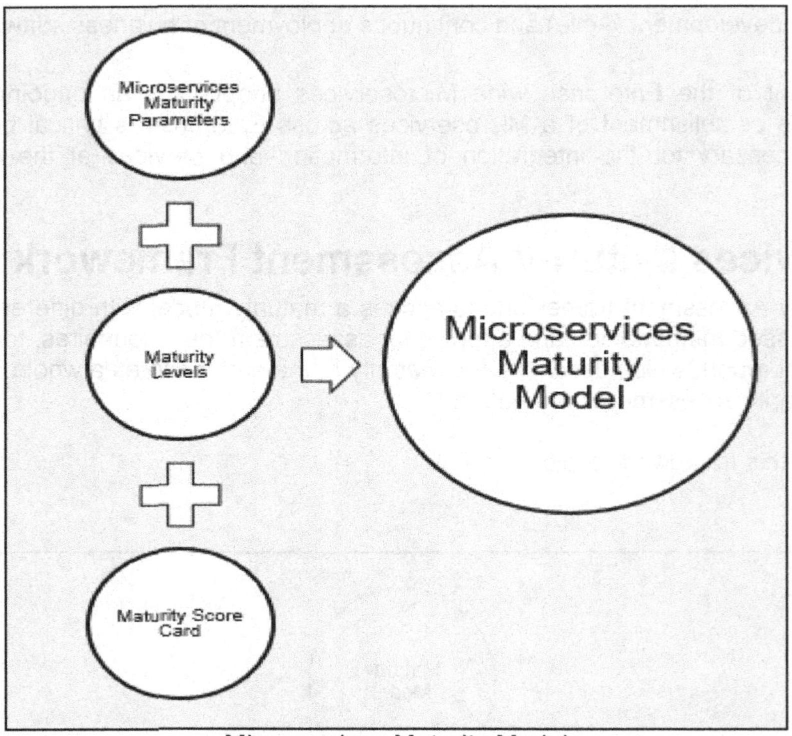

Microservices Maturity Model

The MSMM comprises the following,

- MS Maturity Assessment Parameters
- Microservices Maturity Levels
- Maturity Score Card

9.4 Maturity Model Parameters

Based on our consulting experience in Microservices Maturity assessment and the industry standards, the following Maturity Parameters are used in assessment.

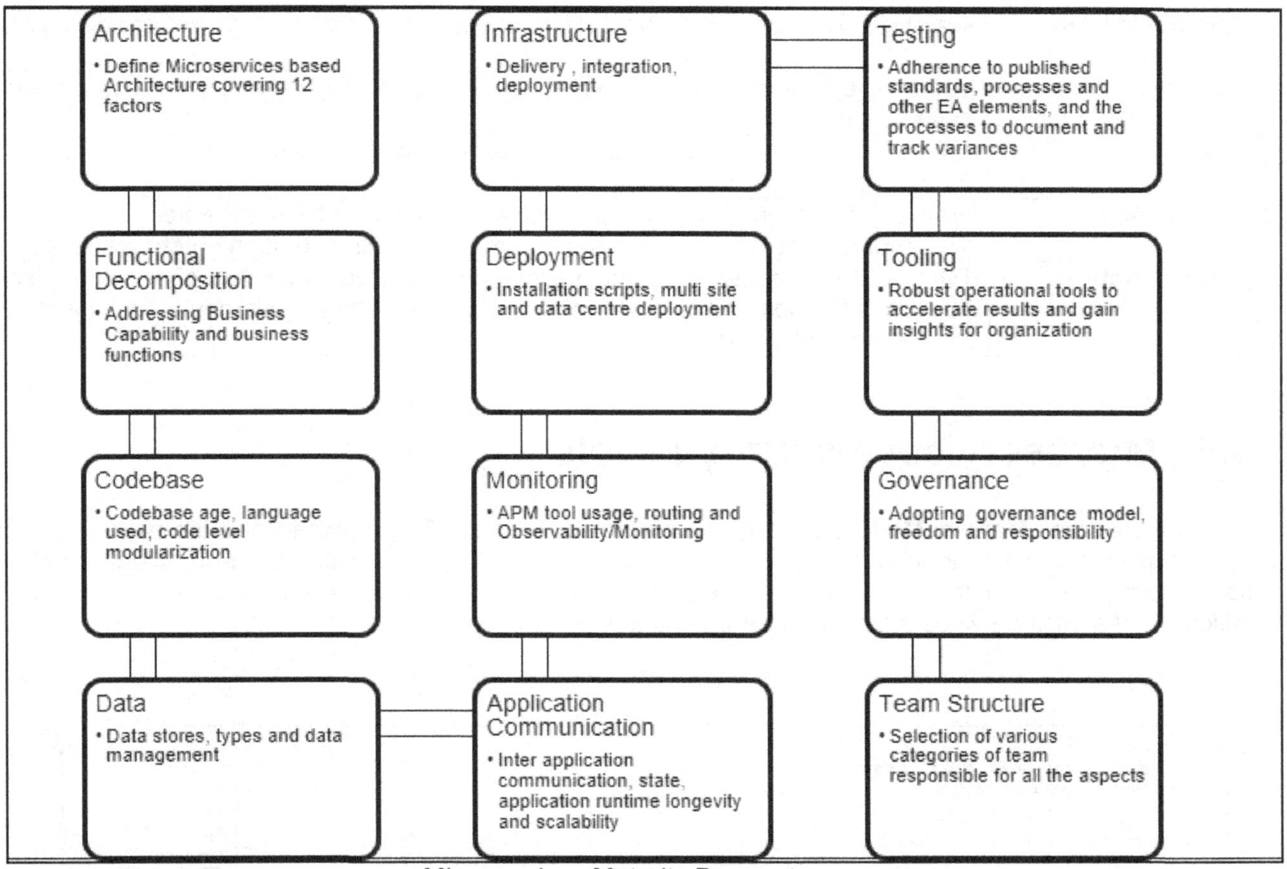

Microservices Maturity Parameters

A brief description of each parameter follows.

Microservices Maturity Parameters	Description
Architecture	This parameter covers Microservices based Architecture covering, 1) architectures and architecture disciplines, 2) architecture perspectives, 3) architecture requirements, 4) architecture means, 5) organizations and individuals and 6) architecture methods
Functional Decomposition	Addressing Business Capability and business functions, which helps to establish the usecases.
Codebase	This Parameter indicates Codebase age, language used, code level modularization. It also provides the typical code coupling and cohesion characteristics
Data	This parameter helps to assess Data stores, data store types and data management.
Infrastructure	It covers Infrastructure related to delivery, integration, deployment and governance parameters
Deployment	This parameter addresses deployment platforms, deployment fabric, deployment artifacts and deployment orchestration. Artifacts are typically, Installation scripts, multi-site and data centre deployment. Infrastructure mutability and infrastructure provisioning details verified.
Monitoring	This covers the APM tool usage, routing and Observability/Monitoring. Strong emphasis on detailed, end-to-end monitoring of production systems. Ability to detect and alert on system issues. Sufficient monitoring to be able to do remote runtime diagnosis
Application	Addresses Inter application communication, state, application runtime longevity and

Communication	scalability. Helps to verify application configuration, inter platform service discovery.
Testing	Verifies the level of testing, automated testing for all the environments, component based testing.
Tooling	Robust operational tools to accelerate results and gain insights for enterprise.
Governance	Architecture governance is the practice and orientation by which enterprise architectures and other architectures managed, controlled at an enterprise-level.
Team Structure	Type of teams necessary to adopt Microservices at various levels of the enterprise. Team has freedom to select technology choices, through governed process and then responsible for its consequences.

9.5 Microservices Maturity Levels

The Microservices Maturity Model and its levels are depicted below. The model follows the path of an enterprise as their Micorservices adoption matures, and sets benchmarks to measure the performance and path that is a natural progression in the development of enterprise architecture. Each level contains statements that are indicative of a Microservices adoption Program at that level.

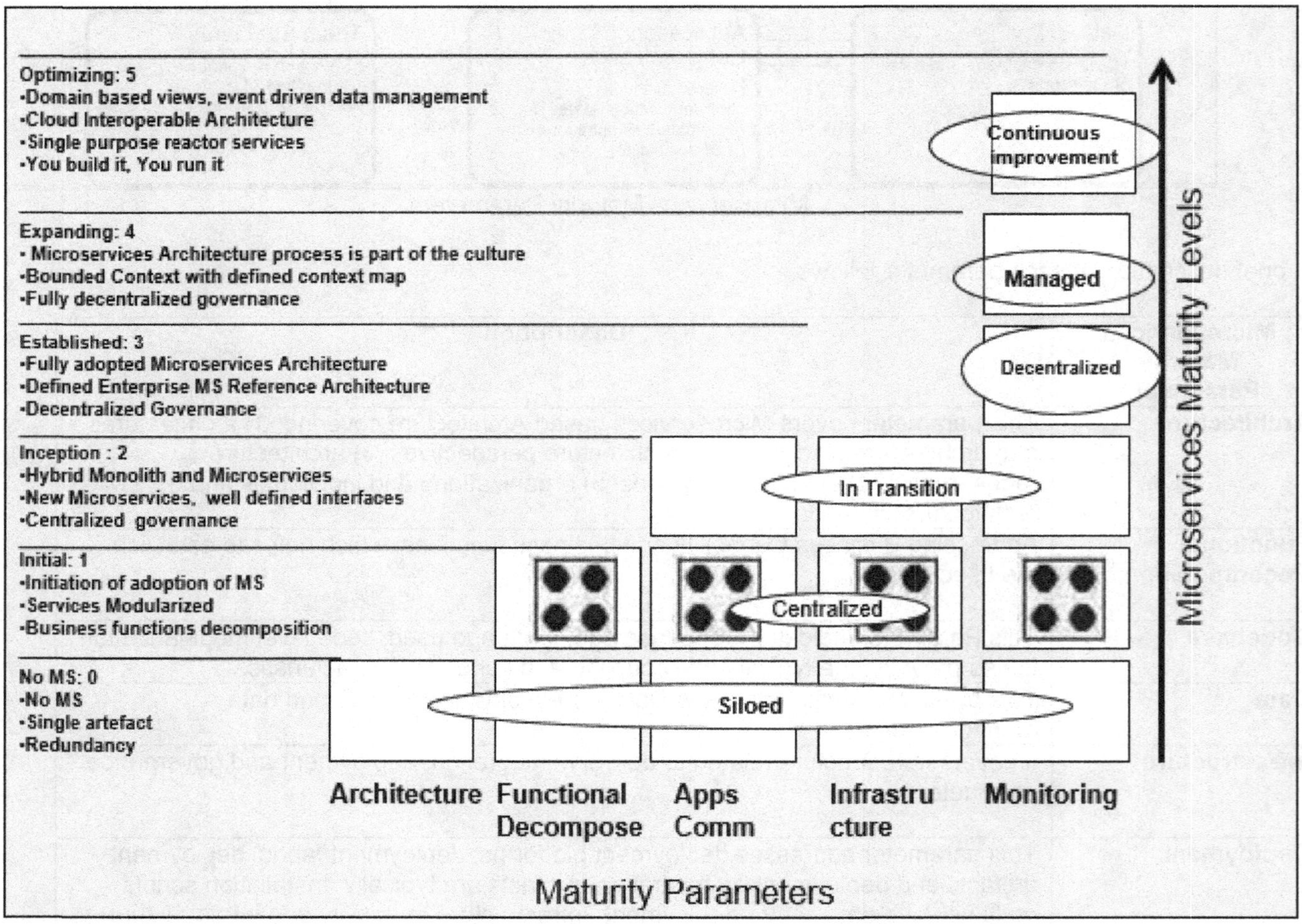

Enterprise Maturity Levels

Level	Description
Level 0: No Microservices	Enterprise still develop applications in a monolithic approach. There is no a documented Microservices in place at this level of maturity. While solutions are developed and implemented, done with no recognized standards or base practices.

Level 1: Initial	The base Microservices architecture framework and standards defined, typically performed informally.
Level 2: Inception	Define hybrid monolithic and Microservices. New Microservices were developed. Manage Governance Centrally
Level 3: Established	Define enterprise Microservices Reference Architecture using approved standard and/or customized versions of the templates. Initiate decentralized governance
Level 4: Expanding	Collect Microservices performance metrics, analyze and acted up on. Metrics used to predict the performance and provide better understanding of the Microservices across the enterprise. Fully decentralized governance.
Level 5: Optimizing	The Microservices architecture processes are mature. Domain based views, event driven data management are established. There are ongoing refinements and improvements based on the understanding of the impact changes have to these processes.

9.6 Maturity Assessment Methodology

The following diagram depicts the Microservices Maturity assessment approach used at Enterprise:

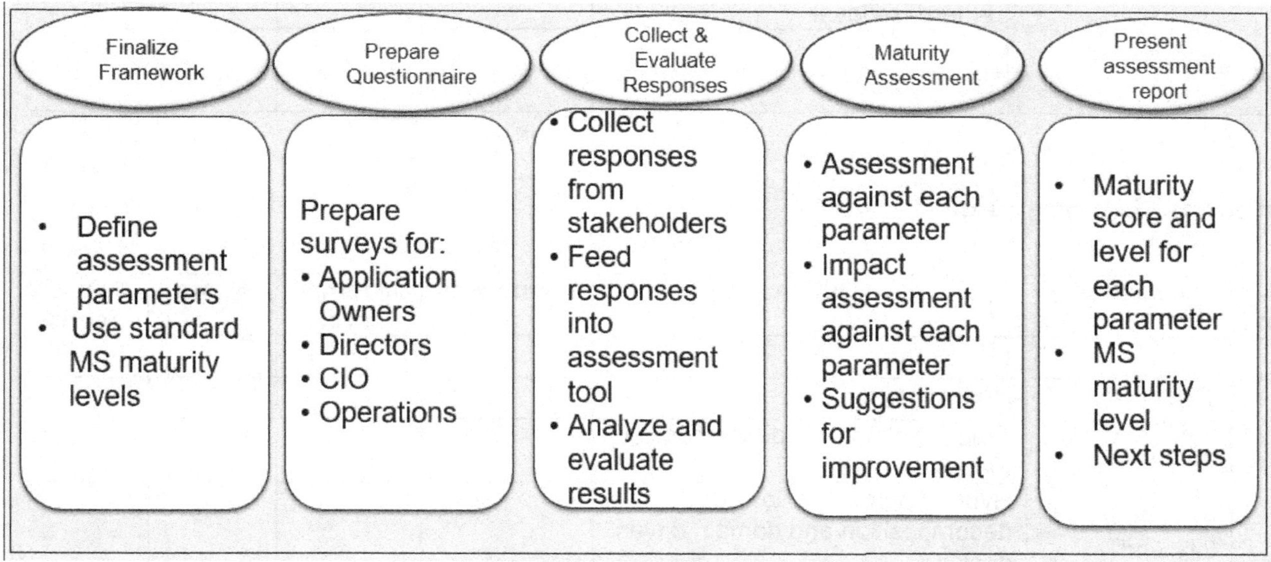

Assessment Methodology

Architecture

Sr. No.	Question	Options	Responses	Maturity level	Score	Maturity scores
1	What is the architecture model the organization is following?	No specific architecture model				
		Monolith architecture				
		Componentized and Layered				
		Services Oriented				
		Hybrid (in transition)				
		Microservices				

2	Is there any formal training provided to the team about Microservices architecture?	No formal training				
		Combination of in house and self learning				
		Formal In house training from designated training department				
		External training with no certification				
		External training with certification				
		Well defined training program in place				
3	What is the outlook for Microservices?	Not going for Microservices				
		Will wait till Microservices mature				
		Will go for partial implementation (where ever applicable)				
		Will go with hybrid approach				
		Implement Microservices at enterprise level				

Functional Decomposition

Sr. No.	Question	Options	Responses	Maturity level	Score	Maturity scores
1	What is the functional domain modelling technique followed	No technique				
		Traditional domain decomposition followed				
		Hybrid approach followed (domain decomposition and domain driven design)				
		Domain driven design followed partially (in one of the departments)				
		Domain driven design followed at enterprise level				
		???				
2	Does team underwent training for domain driven design	No formal training				
		Combination of in house and self-learning				
		Formal In house training from designated training department				
		External training with no certification				
		External training with certification				

		Well defined training program in place				
3	How do entities that span across bounded contexts are finalized	Entities are replicated				
		Follow hybrid model (few replicated and few follow domain driven design)				
		Follow domain driven design modelling				

Code base

Sr. No.	Question	Options	Responses	Maturity level	Score	Maturity scores
1	How is the codebase held	No repository exists, stored locally				
		Stored in centralized repository				
		Hybrid model (centralized or distributed)				
		Distributed (or localized)				
2	What is the codebase age	10+ Years				
		5+ Years				
		3-5 Years				
		1-3 Years				
		New				
3	What is the code level modularization	None				
		Basic Componentization (like packages etc)				
		Componentized at platform level				
		Hybrid of Monolith and Microservices platforms (distributed in later case)				
		Highly componentized				
4	What is the level of code cohesion	Low				
		Low-Medium				
		Medium-High				

		High				

Data

Sr. No.	Question	Options	Responses	Maturity level	Score	Maturity scores
1	What kind of data stores used across enterprise?	Single, External				
		Multiple, External				
		Multiple enterprise data stores				
		Localized data stores (per bounded context)				
		Localized data stores (per Microservice)				
2	What are various data store types used across enterprise?	RDMS, Flat file				
		RDBMS, Search Indexes (like Solr, ElasticSearch)				
		RDBMS, Search Indexes (like Solr, ElasticSearch) and data grids				
		RDBMS, Search Indexes (like Solr, ElasticSearch), NoSQL and lightweight data grids				
		NoSQL				
3	What kind of data model is in place?	Each application has it own data model				
		Canonical model in place for the enterprise				
		Each department has its own data model				
		Data model is semi distributed				
		Data model is decentralized				
4	What kind of data architecture practiced?	Traditional architecture (reads and writes together) on RDBMS				
		Traditional architecture (reads and writes together) on No SQL DBs				
		CQRS on RDBMS				
		CQRS on NO SQL DBs				
		Lambda Architecture				

Infrastructure

Sr. No.	Question	Options	Responses	Maturity level	Score	Maturity scores
1	What is hardware model used?	Traditional racks				
		Virtual machines				
		Containers				
		Hybrid				
2	What is the load balancer infrastructure?	Hardware, centralized				
		Hardware, de-centralized				
		software de-centralized				
		Hybrid approach				
3	Is infrastructure provisioning automated?	Automated				
		Hybrid				
		Manual				
4	Is hadrware monitoring and alerting mechanism available?	Basic, manual tracking and altering				
		Moderate, semi automated mechanism available				
		Fully automated				
5	Is there a provision to monitor application health and lifecycle status?	Individual teams monitor their applications				
		Each department has centralized monitoring				
		Centralized monitoring across applications				

Deployment

Sr. No.	Question	Options	Responses	Maturity level	Score	Maturity scores
1	Is the deployment process automated	No				
		Sometimes				
		Yes				
2	Are there	Yes				

	monitoring and reporting process in place to proactively notify if a deployment fails.	Sometimes (for few applications)				
		No				
3	Is continuous integration used?	Yes				
		No				
		Sometimes				
4	Is build promotion (from one stage to the other) automated?	Yes				
		No				
5	Is there any binary or artefacts repository used for build management	Yes				
		No				

Monitoring

Sr. No.	Question	Options	Responses	Maturity level	Score	Maturity scores
1	Is there any business reference architecture being used as a guideline for specific project implementation?	No				
		Yes				
2	Is there any application reference architecture being used as a guideline for specific project implementation?	No				
		Yes				
3	Is there any data	No				

	reference architecture being used as a guideline for specific project implementation?	Yes				
4	Is there any technology reference architecture being used as a guideline for specific project implementation?	No				
		Yes				
5	Do many of the programming activities include the use of open source software products?	Significant portions are Open Source based				
		Some portions are Open Source based				
		Few portions are Open Source based				
		No portions are Open Source based				
6	Are software systems shared within enterprise?	Not shared at all				
		Shared intra-department but not inter-department				
		Shared inter-department				
7	Are hardware components shared within enterprise?	Not shared at all				
		Shared intra-department but not inter-department				
		Shared inter-department				
8	Are network components shared within enterprise?	Not shared at all				
		Shared intra-department but not inter-department				
		Shared inter-department				

Application Communication

Sr. No.	Question	Options	Responses	Maturity level	Score	Maturity scores
1	Select all those who participate in project prioritization	No formal project prioritization process				
		Ad-hoc and localized process is defined				
		Only technical teams participate				
		Technical teams and architecture representatives participate				
		Technical teams, architects and business teams participate				
		Fully formal process happens through PMO and senior management is kept informed				
2	Who all are involved in Microservices adoption activities?	No enterprise-wide effort.				
		Localized individual support of Enterprise Architecture process. Architecture is project focused.				
		Limited organizational involvement. Architecture exists independently in LoB or geographic silos.				
		Majority of organization is involved. Architecture is federated with defined corporate and LoB responsibilities. However, LoBs and corporate architecture programs do not have coordinated processes & governance.				

		Cross-enterprise architecture involvement. Architecture is unified or federated with standardized corporate and LoB processes and governance structures.				
		Entire organization uses feedback on the architecture process to improve its process. Architecture is unified or federated across the enterprise and encompasses interactions with business partners.				
3	To what extent is senior management involved in the establishment and ongoing development of Microservices?	No management team awareness or involvement in the architecture process.				
		Limited management team awareness or involvement in the architecture process.				
		Occasional/selective management team involvement in the architecture process with various degrees of commitment.				
		Senior-management team aware of and supportive of the enterprise-wide architecture process. Management actively supports architectural standards.				
		Senior-management team directly involved in the architecture review process.				

		Senior-management team directly involved in the optimization of the enterprise-wide architecture development process and governance.				
4	How are these activities apportioned between business and IT today?					

Testing

Sr. No.	Question	Options	Responses	Maturity level	Score	Maturity scores
1	How are metrics used in regards to the integration between management processes and EA?	No measurement mechanism in place				
		Metrics have been defined but are not used				
		Informal review process is in place				
		Metrics are used to measure savings in cost or time				
		Metrics are used to measure savings in cost and time both				
		Metrics are used to proactively identify improvements to the EA framework or blueprint information and/or integration processes				
2	What are the quality assurance metrics that we have?	No metrics in place				
		Need for metrics has been identified				
		Informal review in place - based on points of interest or concern				

		Some metrics are calculated and reviewed formally				
		A measurement and reporting program in place that delivers one report to all stakeholders.				
		A mature, established and planned EA measurement and reporting program that is delivering well crafted messages specific to each key stakeholder, which is continuously reviewed and updated.				
3	Select all who have access to quality measurement data	Quality is not measured				
		Quality is measured but no defined policy for sharing of metrics				
		Quality is measured and policy exists for sharing of metrics but metrics are not shared				
		Quality is measured and policy exists for sharing of metrics but metrics are shared only partially				
		Quality is measured and policy exists for sharing of metrics; metrics are shared with all the relevant stakeholders				
		The organization is taking necessary steps to improve the quality after analysing metrics				

Governance

Sr. No.	Question	Options	Responses	Maturity level	Score	Maturity scores
1	Are Microservices	Not shared at all				
		Shared intra-department				

	adoption Policies, Procedures and Standards shared within enterprise?	but not inter-department				
		Shared inter-department				
2	How often does the architecture team meet and what are the usual means of communication?	No documentation is available.				
		Little communication exists about the Enterprise Architecture process and possible process improvements.				
		The Sharepoint Portal is updated periodically and is used to document architecture deliverables. Communication about architecture process via meetings, etc., may happen, but sporadic. Few tools (e.g., office suite, graphics packages) are used to document architecture.				
		Architecture documents updated and expanded regularly on Sharepoint. Periodic presentations to IT staff on Architecture process, content. Tools are used to support maintaining architecture documentation.				
		Architecture documents are updated regularly, and frequently reviewed for latest architecture developments/standards. Regular presentations to IT staff on architecture content.				
		Architecture documents are used by every decision maker				
3	Are there any Microservices awareness activities conducted frequently across	No education.				
		Limited education.				
		Architecture education done for IT staff.				
		More widespread education done across various Operating Units.				

	enterprise? Do we have a KM repository in enterprise today?	Most Operating Units participate actively in Enterprise Architecture education. Ongoing education on the value of an Enterprise Architecture across Operating Units.				
		All Operating Units participate in staff education and understanding of IT Architecture. Various education/communication tools utilized across all Operating Units.				
4	How would we best describe the growth or change in view of Microservices in campus?					

9.7 Maturity Score Card

The Maturity Score Card describes the maturity scores with respect to each of the Microservices architecture parameters and their maturity level on basis of the maturity assessment exercise, conducted across the enterprise. The following diagram depicts the sample Maturity scorecard.

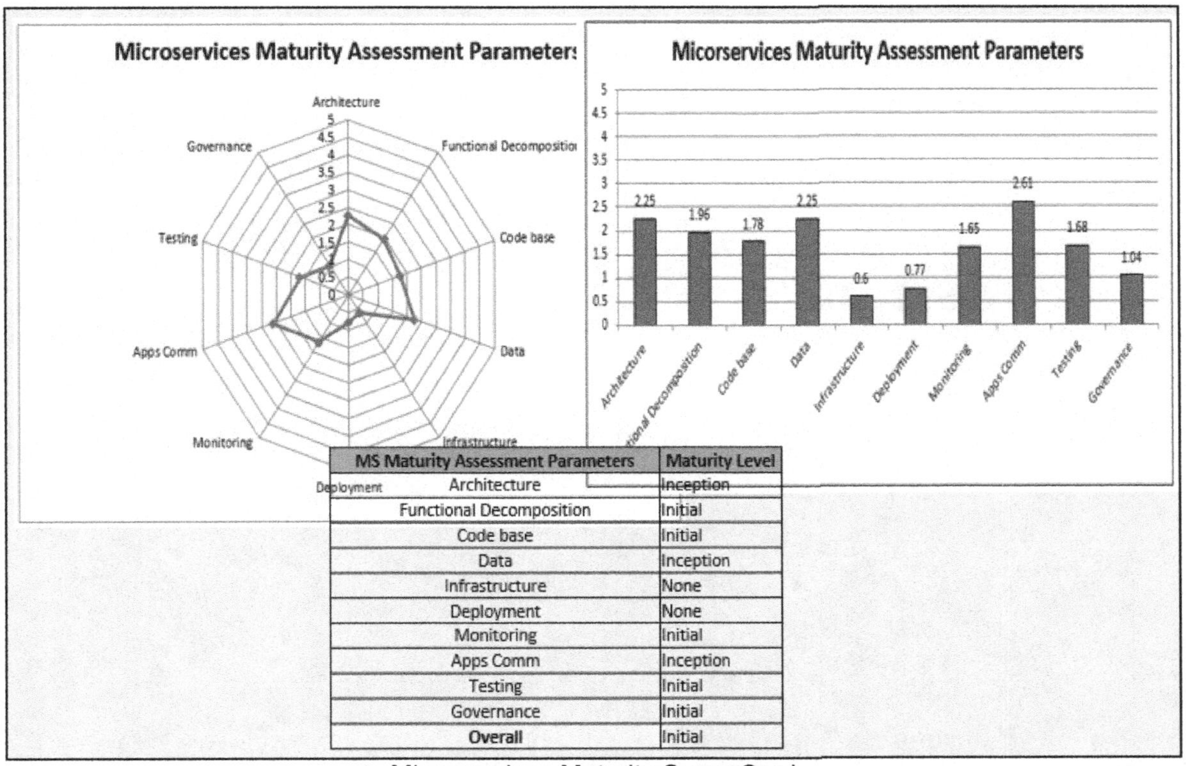

MS Maturity Assessment Parameters	Maturity Level
Architecture	Inception
Functional Decomposition	Initial
Code base	Initial
Data	Inception
Infrastructure	None
Deployment	None
Monitoring	Initial
Apps Comm	Inception
Testing	Initial
Governance	Initial
Overall	Initial

Microservices Maturity Score Card

9.8 Summary

Microservices Maturity within the architecture framework will vary across the business capability, technology architecture, deployment, testing, infrastructure and monitoring as well as the architecture blueprint. This is an ever-evolving process of Enterprise that leads to an efficient, effective responsive development and support organization.

The Microservices Reference architecture blueprint is not a document that we produce once, store on the shelf and reference on occasion. It is a plan and a methodology and allows for better analysis for future decisions. To achieve success with Microservices, enterprises must first build a well-designed application according to existing platform standards; refactor the application into a collection of Microservices as necessary to meet business needs. With the right people, processes, and tools, Microservices can deliver faster development and deployment, easier maintenance, improved scalability, and freedom from technology locking.

The most important parameters considered in the Microservices adoption are:

- Refactoring Existing Applications
- Service Identification
- Technology choices
- Framework choices
- Patterns and integration
- Deployment Automation
- Monitoring, Troubleshooting and Management

10. Best Practices and Conclusion

No legacy system can be transformed into Microservices overnight. Organizations that want to introduce Microservices have to decide where and how these Microservices can be integrated into their existing applications. The first step is to define a Microservices architecture. It has to be established how the services will interact with each other before a company attempts to optimize their implementation. Once Microservices architecture gets going, we have to be able to optimize the increase in speed.

It's better to start with few number of coarse-grained but self-contained services. Fine-graining can happen as the implementation matures over time. To the developer, operations, and testing fraternity who have extensive experience in monoliths, a Microservices-based system is a new reality; hence, they need time to cope with this new shift. Do not discard the monolithic application immediately. Instead, have it co-exist with the new Microservices, and iteratively deprecate similar functionalities in the monolithic application.

It's not easy, and requires a significant investment in people and processes to get started. As with any technology, it's always better to avoid the big-bang approach, and identify ways to get the toes wet before diving in head first.

Always adopt automated toolsets that need to be added to the stack. Granular monitoring, log aggregation and dashboard, application metrics and automated deployment and system dashboard need to be addressed as part of the automated toolset.

The number of best practices for designing and implementing Microservices are,

Business capability based design: Microservices architecture typically needs teams that specialize in particular business capabilities with different requirements, such as order approval, shipping, delivery and returns management, which are all part of order fulfillment. Companies should aim to focus not on more projects, but on products. Services should be developed as independent products that are well documented and each only responsible for a single business capability.

New Features: Identify new features that have to be added to the monolithic application, and develop them instead as Microservices. Alternatively, if new features cannot be identified, it is desirable to replace features in the monolithic application that are "less-critical" and more "self-contained."

New Microservice: Agree on a standard interface for communication between the monolithic application and the new Microservice. The new Microservices needs to be self-contained, and hence, has to have its own runtime environment. The service also needs to be deployed on a separate infrastructure that is isolated, either physically or logically, from the monolithic application

Granularity: Agree on building coarse-grained services which are more actively or frequently used, rather than a bunch of fine-grained services. The coarse grained services will lead to fewer network calls being made between the monolithic application and the Microservices.

Separate data store for each Microservice: Do not use the same data store for all Microservices. Each Microservices team should select the database that is best suited to its service. A single data store also holds a significant risk that Microservices from different teams share the same database structures, perhaps to avoid duplicating work. When one team updates its database structure, other services that use the same structure may also have to be adapted

Code Maturity: All code in a Microservice should have a similar degree of maturity and stability. To add or rewrite the code that works well in a Microservice, the best way is usually to create a new Microservice for the new or altered code and leave the existing Microservice where it is. This allows to iteratively release and test the new code until it is error-free and maximally efficient

Deployment in containers: Deploying Microservices in containers is important, need one tool to deliver everything. As long as the Microservice is in a container, the tool knows how to deliver it. Docker has currently become the standard for containers.

Monitoring: Use logs such as Splunk and monitoring tools like AppDynamics to measure efficiently and simply with mechanisms such as response time notifications, service error notifications and dashboards.

The following table summarise the tools and frameworks that need to be adopted in design to deploy of the Microservices.

Name	Type	Load Balancing	Event Sourcing	Asynchronous Messaging	Service Discovery	Service Monitoring	Proxy Server	NoSQL	CQRS	CI / CD	Persistency	Data	Provisioning	Error handling	API Design	API Analytics	API Gateway	API Management	Authentication	Container Management	Container
Akka	Microservice development	X	X	X																	
Ambassador Gateway	API Management																X				
AMQP	Messaging			X																	
AngularJs	Web Application Development																				
APICur	API Management														X						
Apigee (Google)	API Management														X	X	X	X			
Avro	Messaging			X								X									
AWS CloudFormation	IaaS												X								
AWS DynamoDB	IaaS							X			X										
Blueprint	API Management														X						
Cassandra	Datastorage										X										
Chef	DevOps									X											
Cloudant	Datastorage							X													
Consul	Service Mesh	X			X	X															
Couchbase	Datastorage							X			X										
Datadog	Monitoring					X															
Datomic	Datastorage										X										
DC/OS	Microservices Management																				
Debezium	Datastorage											X									
Docker	Microservices Management																			X	X
Dropwizard	Microservice development																				
ECS (Amazon)	Microservices Management																				
EFS	Security											X									
Envoy	Service Mesh																				
Etcd	Service Mesh				X																
Eureka	Service Mesh				X																
EventStore	Datastorage		X					X													

Eventuate	Microservice development		X						X												
Finagle (Twitter)	Messaging			X																	
Github	DevOps									X											
Gloo	API Management																X				
Graphite	Monitoring																				
Gravitee	API Management														X	X	X	X			
HAProxy	Service Mesh	X					X														
Hyperbahn	Service Mesh				X																
Hystrix (Netflix)	Service Mesh													X							
Istio	Service Mesh	X				X															
Jenkins	DevOps									X											
Jersey	Microservice development																				
JWT	Security																		X		
Kafka (Apache)	Messaging			X								X									
Kubernetes	Microservice s Management																			X	
KumuluzEE	Microservice development				X	X									X						
Lagom	Microservice development																				
LinkerD (Twitter)	Service Mesh				X																
Marathon	Microservice s Management	X			X								X								
MariaDB	Datastorage																				
Mesos (Apache)	Microservice s Management																				
MongoDB	Datastorage							X			X										
MQTT	Messaging			X																	
Nagios	Monitoring					X															
Nelson	Service Mesh																				
Neo4J	Datastorage											X									
Netty	Messaging						X														
NGINX	Messaging	X					X														
Ninja Web Framework	Microservice Development																				
NodeJs	Microservice Development																				
NSQ	Service Mesh				X																
OAuth2.0	Security																				
OpenAPI	API Management														X						
OpenID	Security																				

OpenShift	Microservices Management																				
OpenWhisk	Serverless																				
Pact Framework	DevOps																				
Phabrictor	DevOps																				
Play framework	Microservice development			X																	
Prometheus	Monitoring																				
Protobuf (Google)	Messaging			X								X									
Puppet	DevOps																				
RabbitMQ	Messaging			X																	
RAML	API Management														X						
Rancher	Microservices Management																				
React	Web Application Development																			X	
Redux	Datastorage																				
RestExpress	Microservice Development																				
Restlet	Microservice Development																				
Restx	Microservice Development																				
Ribbon (Netflix)	Messaging	X																			
S3 (Amazon)	Datastorage											X									
Serf	Service Mesh				X	X															
Service Fabric	PaaS																				
SmartStack	Service Mesh				X	X															
Spring Boot	Microservice development																				
Spring Cloud	Microservice development																				
Spring Cloud Gateway	API Management																X				
Squash	DevOps																				
STOMP	Messaging			X																	
Swagger	API Management																				
Synapse	Service Mesh																				
Thrift (Apache)	Messaging			X								X			X						
Thrift IDL	API Management																				
Traefik	Service Mesh	X					X														
Tyk	API Management														X	X	X				
Vaadin	Web Application Development																				
VueJs	Web Application Development																				
WADL	API Management														X						
Wildfly	Microservice Development																				
Zipkin	DevOps																				
ZooKeeper (Apache)	Microservices Management				X																
Zuul	API Management																X				

About the Authors

Dr. Gopala Krishna Behara is a Distinguished Member of Technical Staff (DMTS) at Wipro Technologies, and currently playing the role of Lead Enterprise Architect of Architecture Group of Wipro. He is certified in Open Group TOGAF, IBM Cloud Solutions. He serves as an Advisory Architect and Mentor on Enterprise Architecture, Application Portfolio Rationalization, Cloud Native Technologies, Architecture Assurance initiatives and continues to work as a Subject Matter Expert and Author. He has worked on multiple IT transformation engagements in the USA, UK, Europe, Asia Pacific and Middle East Regions that presented a phased roadmap to transformation that maximized the business value, while minimizing costs and risks.

Published White Papers, articles and blogs in International Journals in SOA, BPM, Next Generation Technologies & e-Governance space and also done significant contribution for the Cloud Native Architecture definition across the organisation. Published couple of books titled "Enterprise Architecture Practitioner Hand Book" and "Next Generation Enterprise Reference Architecture for Connected Government".

Recipient of EA Hall of Fame - Individual Leadership in EA Practice, Promotion and Professionalisation Award, 13th Annual Enterprise Architecture Conference, Washington, DC, USA – 2015.

Tirumala Khandrika is Senior Architect in the Enterprise Architecture practice of Wipro. Has 17 years of experience in software engineering which includes software architecture, design and development for internet/intranet, client server applications and business application systems for clients in USA, Europe and Asia.

Extensive experience in architecting, designing and developing enterprise and web based applications in BFS, manufacturing, aerospace, healthcare domains using Java/JEE, Spring and SOA platforms Experience in customer relationship and successfully handled engagements in gaining the confidence of the customer.

Review Team

We would to thank following team members for providing feedback and valuable inputs for the book:

Hari Kishan Burle, Vice President and Global Head Architecture Services,Wipro Technologies

Raju Alluri, Global Delivery Head, Global Architecture, Wipro Technologies

Prasad Palli, Lead Enterprise Architect, Architecture, Wipro Technologies

Disclaimer

Made in United States
North Haven, CT
05 November 2026

21763978R00083